SUNSTONE ANGEL PUBLISHING™
High Prairie, Alberta CANADA

ISBN-13: 978-1515206941
ISBN-10: 1515206947

FIRST EDITION
SUNSTONE ANGEL PUBLISHING™

For more information about permission to reproduce selections from this book, please contact the author at dq@sunstoneangel.com.

Book design by Rocky Berlier
Manufactured in the United States of America

ABOUT A Blue Angel

by DIANE QUARTLY

Dedication

To my "little man," Travis, who allowed me to know him better in six years than most parents know their children in sixty.

To my "big men" Levi and Devon, who gave me reason to get up and keep going every day. You make me extremely proud of the kind and wonderful men you've become.

To my "main man" Arlen, for so many happy, wonderful and love filled years. Forever & Always.

To my parents, Arne and Charlene, for sharing their love and respect.

To "June", for enduring such sadness. In order for one to forgive they would have to have laid blame. I have no need to forgive as I have never felt blame, *ever*. I wish you always only love.

To my family for the love, laughs and memories.

To my closest friends, for allowing me to be myself in their presence.

Contents

Pre-Foreword

The past empowers the present,
And the groping footsteps leading to this present
mark the pathways to the future.
~Mary Catherine Bateson

You haven't overcome the fear of death until you delight
In your own life, believing it to be the carrying out of
the universal purpose.
~George Bernard Shaw

My father had a leather, hinged box, lined with velvet. Inside was a collection of colorful, round pins. Each of which represented a year of perfect attendance at Sunday School. I only saw it one time, I don't remember why he showed it to me, but it made a lasting impression. The pride he took in these mementos had the emotional weight of an Oscar in my young mind.

Religion and church were important parts of my early life, as I matured I became a Sunday School teacher myself and a lay-reader, a person in the congregation who stands up and reads the Old Testament Lesson during a Sunday service. However, as I aged into a teenager and had a questioning mind I became less content with the doctrine of my beloved Saint Francis of Assisi Episcopal Church. I wanted more.

What is the soul? Is reincarnation real? Can we connect with our departed loved ones? Do angels really protect us and bring us messages? Sadly for me, my church didn't have answers for my burning desired questions. And so, I began my own quest.

I went to various churches with friends and their families. I read everything I could get my hands on: philosophy, eastern thought, meditation, new thought, and on and on. Back in that day, I researched whatever was available.

Billy Graham had written a book on angels. It seemed a safe bridge between my Christian foundation and what I was longing for, a more personal connection to the Creator. My search and open mind took me to places I couldn't anticipate, satisfying and beautiful, heart-filling places. So, when I was contacted by Diane Quartly to read her manuscript, *ABOUT A BLUE ANGEL*, I was intrigued and excited.

This is a true story of joy, disbelief, adjustment, shock, grief and ultimately grace, *"the peace that passeth no understanding"*.

After marriage to her sweetheart and the birth of their first healthy son, Diane and Arlen had no reason to be concerned about the health of their next beautiful boy. However, son number two was special, different and with mental adjustment they faced Travis' special needs with loving-kindness. Soon, the stork brought baby number three another healthy boy. Life continued, with each family member's needs addressed as in all families. Until one day when the unthinkable happened.

The human reactions, the blessings, the anger, the betrayal and once again the grace that seasons this story will, I believe, compel, inspire and leave you with your own sense of peace. We are resilient, we humans, we can face what comes, learn, grow and rise above the difficulties into a collaboration with Source. That is the place where we can joyfully dance with the angels.

I believe that you will close this book after reading the final page with a sigh and a smile, grateful that you took the time to get to know this family. I know I am.

~ *Cynthia Richmond*
Author of The Dream Power Journal
www.DreamPower.net

Foreword

L ife is rarely, if ever, without the call from Spirit to face a contrast of experiences; how we wish them to be versus how they play out. These dark moments of our Soul are a paradox and beautiful mixture of good and bad, light and dark, happy and sad. We must have both day & night, masculine & feminine, movement & stillness, right brain & left brain, focus & flexibility; both sides of the coin to complete the circle of life, rich in content, wholeness and great purpose.

The Universe asks us to first bring one and then other into light and learn to flow with the rhythm and *interconnectedness* of all things and each other. It is a dynamic interplay between the powerful pairs of duality that allows the ebb and flow, which are essential for life and for growth.

When I first met Diane a few years ago, I was immediately captivated by the compassion and grace in which she expressed life in the midst of a painful reality most of us cannot even contemplate. The death of a child is the most devastating loss and to uncover light in one of the most unthinkable moments is truly a gift that runs deep into the human spirit. A parent mourns the loss of his or her life, potential and future. It is a degree of suffering that is impossible to grasp. Diane brings light to grief through sharing the story of her son's short life as a pendulum swing of love.

Challenges are a part of life. Diane shows her eternal human humbled by the beauty and complexity of her own strength to survive, rise above, to learn and begin again.

This is a story of darkness and light, about sorrow and joy and the celebration of a little boy and his soul's purpose. It is real life; utterly tragic in beautiful healing glory. A mother's struggle to restore her capacity to love and find reason and clarity that truly magnifies the significance of every lesson and every person. A story that makes a positive contribution to the development and advancement of the human race; it opens minds and opens hearts to love again.

This is an inspiring story that illustrates one can get through the most challenging of ordeals and come out happy on the other side. Life is forever changed and as Diane shares through the intricately woven story of Travis, it is not over. It truly is a brilliant portrayal of a mother's choice and determination to not let her sorrow become her child's legacy.

ABOUT A BLUE ANGEL honor's Travis' memory and inspires us all to carry on through what seems so impossible and to begin again. It is defined by character, illumination of gifts, and through courage to the end, which can only be explained as Divinity in action. This is an exceptional story of a "forever" connection that is available to all of us through love; nowhere and everywhere at the same time.

It is hope that keeps individuals persevering through the turbulent times and with extraordinary grace and faith rise above stronger and more 'in love' than ever before.

~Bonnie Wirth
Co-Author of HEART TO HEART: THE PATH TO WELLNESS
http://www.bonniewirth.net

Acknowledgements

I thank God and my beautiful team of Angels and Guides for supporting me with love as I make my way through this physical life.

I am so very grateful for my human team players:

Dawn McConnell for answering that first call from my "little man".

Bonnie Wirth for pointing me in the direction of my life purpose.

Cynthia Richmond for being the cheerleader that dreams are made of.

Rocky Berlier for helping me release the unnecessary and focus on what is important.

To all of the above, I appreciate and thank you for the beautiful inspiration you are to me!

INTRODUCTION

Lost and Found

I have lived through one of the worse things any person could live through, and yet, I am blessed by the experience. I have hurt, I have grieved and I have found comfort in knowing that something larger than this life does exist, and it is now so completely part of my life.

Sixteen years ago, my life changed in the matter of about 10 seconds. An incident that so many others have experienced happened to my family and me. And in the aftermath of it, I found myself on a path of self-discovery that would change my life and my world forever.

Why did this happen? What did I do to deserve this? What do I do now? I wanted to know and I searched every book and article, every TV show and movie, for anything similar or anyone who had gone through the same thing. I was looking for and hoping to find what I had lost by connecting with others who had gone through such a loss. In doing so, I found a new life.

I didn't have to change what I believed; I just started to "pay attention" to what I knew to be true. I found many books about loss and grief and articles about God and the creation of life. I found stories that filled my heart and made me realize that I was not alone, but there was never enough. I am writing this story, my story, so that those who are seeking will find one more connection in their search for familiarity, their search for comfort.

I found my way to a world of forgiveness and truth, of love and light, and now I am at a place in my journey where I am able to help others, even just a little bit, to find peace and happiness and answers to their questions.

I am a psychic medium and I give people the gift of connecting with their loved ones and in return, I receive such an amazing gift of truth and a deeper connection to Source. I acknowledge that my life is still a work in progress, it is never complete, for when it is, that is the day my life is over. Until then, I get up each morning and give thanks to God for all the blessings in my life and I lay down at night knowing that I did my best that day. I am forever changing, growing, learning, exploring and I am excited beyond measure about what is unfolding along the path I have chosen.

Life is so beautiful and precious. I am determined to help people realize that no matter how bad their lives seem to be, there is always a way to feel a little bit better than you did a moment ago. Through my work I have come to realize that our job in this lifetime is simple; to find joy and happiness.

My sincerest desire is to help people through the sharing of my story. I want it to give them hope and healing for their broken hearts, to serve as a support that they are not alone, that we are not alone. I want it to confirm, affirm and validate that life truly goes on beyond this plane of existence and that our loved ones see us, hear us and have amazing insights and guidance for us. We are living in a blessed world if we just shift our perspective, our consciousness and pay attention.

~Diane Quartly

CHAPTER 1

Angels

My obsession with angels and the afterlife started well before 1999, however, an important event occurred that year, which certainly brought these things to the forefront of my life.

I wasn't raised in a religious family and my only association with religious concepts was the little bit that I was taught in school by way of the Easter bunny and Christmas pageants. Perhaps, it was those times in class that made me accept that there was a God or maybe I just always knew. I know now one thing is for certain, there exists a Source that is connected to us all, every minute of everyday, and at all times.

I was never a fan of scary movies, books or anything that could be considered negative and I always loved angels. I remember how thrilled I was to be an angel in the story of "Mary and Joseph" the one year I attended the Christmas service at my aunts' church along with her, my uncle and cousins. They let me put on the long white gown and I was giddy with excitement over the halo made of wire wrapped in tinsel. I was only about 10 years old, but remember it like it was yesterday.

Fast forward to 1999 and my fascination with angels became so much more. At that time, I began to read, in earnest, all there was available about the angels, archangels and the roles that they played in our everyday life. By the summer of 2000, I was addicted to a new show on TV called *Crossing Over with John Edward*. Here was a guy that stood in a room and communicated with people who have died, connecting them with their loved ones, who so desperately needed comfort and validation. It was amazing to watch and I was hooked.

I especially loved anything written by Sylvia Brown at the time and found her insights into the spirit realm fascinating. My cousin Debbie, who was just as interested in angels, and I managed to get tickets to see her live and I so wanted a reading, but it didn't happen.

About the same time, my husband, Arlen, and I decided to take a trip to Toronto for a weekend to attend a John Edward show and I remember praying all the way there that I would get a reading.

As we entered the auditorium, my heart sank as I noticed the large number of people attending the event. So many people were there hoping to connect with passed loved ones. Arlen and I took our seats, which were close to the middle of the auditorium. It was warm, so I removed my jacket and turned around to lay it over the back of my chair. As I did, I looked over the crowd, which was getting settled-in behind me.

I wondered about their stories; surely mine was not the only broken heart, but was my story important enough to get a reading? I tossed this thought around in my head, contemplating my importance and the importance of my loss. Out of all these people, there must be many more that needed a reading as much as I did; some who perhaps needed one more. I could not imagine that anyone could be feeling as heartbroken as I felt right then, but I knew better; I knew there were people that hurt worse, people that were more desperate, people more lost. I reasoned with myself that I would get a reading if it was meant to be; if I was meant to connect, yet I prayed and I begged God to let John come to me.

The lights went down in the crowd and the stage was lit up. I was anxious beyond words by the time John Edward walked on stage.

I can't recall that show. Little about it stuck in my mind. I was so absorbed in my own loss; in my own need that I was unable to appreciate the miracles of healing happening around me. I was so caught up in my own pleading and praying within my head that I could not hear the messages that were given to those who were blessed.

We left the show disheartened and I felt very sorry for myself. We were so glad we had made the trip to see the show, but it was kind of like enjoying a hockey game, but feeling depressed because your favorite team lost.

I continued to read and study, eventually becoming quite knowledgeable about how I believed the afterlife worked. I began an inner journey into really understanding how my energy works, how our chakras and auras work and I began to meditate regularly.

I didn't believe everything I read. There were many authors who wrote about angels and what they believed about the afterlife didn't resonate with me; it didn't feel right. At first I wanted to believe everything, but somehow, I got to the point where I just knew some things were the authors' interpretation and I could not relate to their ideas. I especially had issues with people that wrote about the negative side of Spirit.

I do not believe that God punishes his children and I do not believe in the Devil. I believe in a loving and gentle God or Source, one that encourages us to experience all that life has to offer, and I recognize that there are consequences for every action we take and what we perceive to be good or bad. If you dwell on the negative, you then create the negative. However, this is another topic of energy and creation that will continue further into this story.

A few years later (at a time when I still searched for answers, but had a much better understanding of certain concepts and what I believed to be true), a friend told me about a lady that was going to be in the next town, about an hour's drive from where I lived. She told me that the lady was a medium and I knew that meant she could connect to people in heaven, to people who had crossed over to that beautiful place I only imagined. I knew I had to see her; I called the number she gave me and made the appointment for two days later.

As I drove to my appointment, my heart was racing, I felt like something big was about to happen. I didn't know what to expect. I had studied all sorts of spiritual and metaphysical experiences, but really, until now, it was all just someone else's; I had no personal, recognizable experience of my own that I could consciously acknowledge.

I had travelled to Toronto to see John Edward and I had travelled to both Edmonton and Calgary to see Sylvia Brown; each time disappointed that I didn't get what they called a "reading". It was wonderful to be in the audience of those shows, but I wanted a personal reading in the biggest way. I wanted to connect.

I pulled up to the address I was given and got out of my minivan. It was summer and that day was warm and beautiful. There was a slight breeze and the air smelled fresh. I walked around to the back of the house like I was instructed too and was met by a lovely lady with intense eyes. She introduced herself as Dawn and I told her my name, just my first name, as I had when I booked the appointment. I saw a table and chairs sitting underneath a large green umbrella and she asked if it would be all right if we sat outside. There was lemonade in a crystal pitcher sitting beside two glasses on top of the tempered glass table, one was half full and one was empty, waiting for me.

The moment I sat down, with thoughts of the cool lemonade on my mind, Dawn looked over at me and gently spoke "He's here."

Since that first reading, and after what felt like a lifetime of my own spiritual evolution and experiences, a full eight years had passed where I was now at the point of being able to give my own readings.

CHAPTER 2

Our Little Man

Nineteen months after the birth of our first son, Levi, our second of three boys arrived in a bit of frenzy on February 8, 1993. From the very first real contraction to the moment he was born, a short time of one hour and 53 minutes had passed. It was a good thing I was already at the hospital for a checkup that day. I remember looking at my son's slim face and big brown eyes and falling in love with him just as quickly as his labor had been. Life never felt better as Arlen and I, married for four years at that time, were welcoming our second son into the family.

Our oldest son, Levi, had been a good baby and such a smart and gentle little boy. We were thrilled to be adding to our family and he was very excited to have a little brother.

That first night with Travis went very well; he was so sweet and did not fuss at all. I woke up every couple of hours to feed him and I hummed to the tune of "Greensleeves" as I stroked the hollow on the bridge of his nose, just as I had with Levi when he was born.

Arlen came to the hospital early the next morning with Levi and it was so adorable to watch Levi kiss his brother's little face and later sit in a chair while we helped support Travis so he could hold him. Grandparents and friends, aunts, uncles and cousins all came to see our new little man and we were proud to show him off.

Our bliss was short lived however, when later that day (the day after Travis was born), our doctor came to tell us that during the post birth assessment, he had noticed signs of a genetic abnormality. Being young and naïve, we were surprised, but not especially worried. After all, our son looked perfect! So what if the lines crisscrossing the palm of his hands and fingers were a little different, or that his ears sat a little low on the side of his head? No one even noticed until it was pointed out. We filled out all the paperwork the next day to start the genetic testing process, and then took our beautiful little boy home; we felt blessed.

Life was pretty normal for the first few weeks. My husband worked and I stayed home with our two little boys. I enjoyed being a mom although it was overwhelming at times. We had set up our little nest and things were going well.

When it came time for both Travis' and my six-week checkup, I was a little nervous because I knew that he had not gained weight like he should have. He was still gaining and doing okay, but he seemed to spit-up quite a bit more than Levi had and would often choke on his milk. I was nursing as I had with Levi, but was concerned that I may have to start supplementing with formula.

The checkup went well and, although the doctor noted the low weight gain, Travis seemed to otherwise be doing fine. Knowing we had an appointment with the geneticist in Edmonton a few weeks later, our doctor decided we should monitor his progress once a week for the next few weeks, if for nothing else, to have a record for the geneticist.

It was during one of these visits that I asked my doctor to do a pregnancy test on me. I had reluctantly taken a home test and it was positive, but I wanted to be sure. It was quite a surprise, considering I was still nursing, to find out just three months after Travis was born, that I was expecting again.

This news was met by very mixed reactions. Most of the family were supportive but a few had concerns, not only because I was having another child so soon after our second, and not even because we were still not sure what we would be dealing with as far as Travis's future, but because of the trouble I had after my first pregnancy with Levi.

A few months into that pregnancy, I had a chemical imbalance that progressed to a full-blown postpartum psychosis after he was born. My world was spinning and spinning out of control fast. I won't tell all the strange stories that I do remember; just know, that from a person who has never taken drugs of any kind, I believe I had the greatest hallucinations one could imagine.

Looking back on it, I remember that I had a symptom that I chose to ignore. Actually, my eye doctor chose to ignore it as well. I had worn contact lenses for about four years with no issues, however, during my pregnancy with Levi, I had to change my lenses a ridiculous amount of times because they kept turning a slight shade of brown around the edges of the lens. The chemicals in my body were changing severely; we should have known something was wrong.

I ended up enduring a three-month hospital stay so doctors could regulate the chemicals in my body. Arlen was left to work and raise Levi (who was less than six months old) on his own during that time. I was so thankful he had help from family, especially his mom. It was a very unpleasant situation and although I remember little of that time in hospital, my family and some dear friends remember all too well how debilitated and out of my right mind I was.

It wasn't long after this, when things finally settled down and I was chemically "back to normal", that I learned I was pregnant with Travis. My family and my doctor watched intensely for any signs of another imbalance. However, all remained well and now, after finding out the little we knew about Travis' genetic prognosis, I was pregnant once again.

A couple more months passed while we adjusted and moved forward with the changes happening in our lives. We had finally finished going through genetic testing to find out exactly what anomalies there may be and what effects they would have on Travis. It was during this time that he began to get a cold, which progressed into bronchitis and then to pneumonia. Our life of visits to the doctors then began. Travis would get better for a time and we would take him home. Then he would get sick again and back to the hospital we would go.

While I nursed him at first, we tried to introduce formula early because he seemed to need the extra nutrition. Nothing we tried worked. Everything he drank would reflux at the back of his throat and gradually end up coming out of his nostrils. It was that pooling in the back of his throat and sinuses that caused the infection and eventual pneumonia several times.

We found out (through further genetic testing of Arlen and me) that a chromosome imbalance called Trisomy 9p with developmental delay existed on my husband's side. Arlen was a carrier of the Trisomy 9 chromosome, but where his 9th and 14th chromosomes split and attached themselves was at a "balanced juncture". Unfortunately, where Travis' split was an unbalanced juncture.

Although they did not know then, nor do they now, very much about this type of disability, the good news was that whatever he was able to do, whatever he was able to accomplish, would be what it was; it would not degenerate and would not get worse over time, as far as they could tell.

I began to research everything I could about this genetic condition.

Chromosome 9, Trisomy 9p is a rare chromosomal syndrome in which a portion of the 9th chromosome appears three times (trisomy) rather than twice in cells of the body. The trisomy may involve a portion of the short arm (9p), the entire short arm, or the short arm and a portion of the long arm (9q) of chromosome 9. (Each chromosome contains a short arm known as "p" and a long arm designated as "q.") Evidence suggests that, in many cases, associated symptoms and findings may be relatively similar among affected infants despite differing lengths of the trisomic (duplicated) segment of 9p. However, in those with larger trisomies (e.g., extending to middle or end [distal] regions of 9q), additional features may also be present that appear to correlate with the extent of the duplication.

Virtually all individuals with Trisomy 9p are affected by mental retardation and distinctive malformations of the skull and facial (craniofacial) region. In some instances, additional physical abnormalities may also be present, such as other skeletal defects, structural malformations of the heart that are present at birth (congenital heart defects), and/or other findings. In some cases, the trisomy appears to result from a balanced chromosomal rearrangement in one of the parents; in others, it is thought to arise from spontaneous (de novo) errors very early in embryonic development that occur for unknown reasons (sporadically).

From : *www.webmd.com*

After a brief period of panic and a little bit of anger and frustration for the anticipated struggles our little man was undoubtedly going to have to deal with, we decided we had better just "suck it up" and remain positive. We never once lost hope; we believed he would be able to do it all!

I was now five months pregnant and as was the case with both of my first two pregnancies, things seemed to be progressing normally. My doctor was watching for signs of any chemical reaction or imbalance and everything seemed to be good; that was until I woke one night to severe pain in my abdomen. I knew something was wrong, but I could still feel my baby move, so I somehow reasoned that he was fine. The pain was intense and it didn't feel like anything else I had ever felt with my other two pregnancies.

Arlen called his mother, who lived the closest, to stay with Levi and Travis while he rushed me to the hospital. It was about a fifteen-minute drive from where we lived and once we arrived at the hospital emergency room, my doctor was called to come from his home. It only took him a couple of minutes to reach the hospital.

After a quick examination, he then mentioned there was a surgical specialist from Edmonton visiting our little hospital that night and my doctor had asked if he would examine me. Within minutes, both doctors decided I needed critical care and they requested a plane to fly me to the city of Edmonton. Both doctors thought that it was possible that my appendix may have burst. Arlen immediately called his parents and told them what was going on and then called my parents to tell them the same.

I was then taken to a small airstrip by ambulance and I remember being strapped down to the bed as they carried me up the steps from the ground into the plane. Everything happened so fast and as I looked out, I saw Arlen, my parents and a few other family members standing by the side of the airstrip looking extremely worried while they waved goodbye. With only the pilot, co-pilot, and nurse on the plane with me, the flight was uneventful and we landed in the city less than an hour later.

After a quick ride to the University Hospital, again by ambulance, I was taken directly to an operating room where about 20 people were waiting. I asked why there were so many people and they said there was a surgical team to do my operation and also a team in case the baby had to be delivered. I was worried and in quite a bit of pain by this time and welcomed the anesthetic to put me to sleep.

By the time my husband made the four-hour drive to the city with my younger sister, Shirley, I was already out of surgery and back in my room. My baby had not been delivered and the surgery had gone well. It wasn't until the next day when a doctor came in to tell me that it wasn't actually my appendix, but rather I had a cyst on my right ovary the size of a grapefruit, which had burst. The doctor told me I was extremely lucky that the cyst had burst inside of my ovary and was contained; otherwise, it could have easily caused an infection for me as well as for my unborn baby. He said they actually had to lift the baby out of the way to remove my right ovary, yet everything had gone well.

I was worried about the anesthesia I'd already been given and the effects of it on my baby. I was totally against taking any unnecessary pain medication during pregnancy and labor. I hadn't had any painkillers with either of my first two labors, so I refused to take any while recovering.

The pain was extreme, but I refused any pain treatment until a doctor came in on the second day of post-op to tell me that the amount of pain my body was in was actually causing the baby *more* distress than if I took a minimal amount of pain medication to take the edge off. I finally agreed and looking back on that day, I'm glad I did what I did, but if I had to do it over again, I'd take the pain meds immediately.

My sister, Shirley, visited for a bit and reported to the rest of the family waiting back in High Prairie (the town we live in, 365 km north of Edmonton) that all was well, and then left me to sleep and recover.

The next day, she caught a ride back to High Prairie and my husband stayed. On the second night, he decided that instead of sitting all night in a hotel room, he would ride along with a grain-hauler friend of his, who was travelling through the city (going south to pick up a load) and would be back through again just after midnight.

My hospital room had four beds. There was a young girl across from me who cried continually, sobbing quietly. The nurse told me that the young girl had the same surgery I had (without the pregnancy part). The lady next to me had a terrible abdominal abscess and slept soundlessly all the time. The last lady who shared our room was an older lady who I was told had cancer. She was very frail and did nothing but sleep. Her family came in each day to visit and I was fortunate enough to witness the love they had for their matriarch.

On my third night, just before 3:00 AM, I awoke to the nurses wheeling-out the older lady in her bed; she was silent and still. I somehow knew she had passed away in her sleep. I was horrified when her family came in to visit her early the next morning. I will never forget her son's face when he saw the empty space where her bed had once been. He turned a questioning look in my direction just as a nurse came in and escorted them to another room. It was heartbreaking.

As bad luck would have it, there was an accident that closed down the highway, which delayed Arlen's return. Usually this would not have made a difference, especially since I was tucked safely in a hospital bed, however, my doctor came in early that morning and discharged me.

So, there I sat, waiting patently for Arlen's return and reflecting on the morning's events regarding the lady who had died. Even though I had no phone, no money, no food, not even shoes or a jacket (from 10 AM when I was discharged, until 6:00 PM when he finally got there), I felt fortunate that my surgery had gone well. I was in pain and had been sitting in the waiting room downstairs at the hospital for all those hours, too young and naïve to make trouble or ask for assistance. I was more than ready to go home when he walked in and I was so happy to see him.

The rest of my pregnancy went well and we continued to learn more about Travis' genetic disorder. Thankfully, my wonderful cousin, Tracy, stayed with us and helped until I recovered from surgery well enough to be able to at least lift-up my other two children.

Devon was born four months later, thankfully without any signs of Trisomy 9p (just under a year after Travis' birth) and he was perfect. He had big blue eyes that have remained blue, and looked so very much like Levi did when he was born. In fact, both Levi and Devon were the exact same weight at birth: 7 lbs 12 oz. Travis was our "little man" at 6 lbs 3 oz.

Once again, life returned to as normal as it could be with three children under four years of age.

CHAPTER 3

Chiropractors & Adjustments

Throughout all of this, my husband continued to play hockey with the local senior team and I was beginning to become close friends with some of the hockey players' wives. It was through this team that Arlen and I met and became friends with Barry, one of the goalies, and his wife, June. She was a young active mom with a daughter a little older than Levi. Their second child, a son, was born just 14 months before Travis. This made it easy for us to become close, since we were both young mothers starting our families.

We would call each other on the phone every day, sometimes talking for hours while we cleaned, did laundry, fed the children and quite often, our families would get together on the weekends to play cards while the kids played. Eventually, I started working part-time at the same real estate office as June and we even became gym buddies.

She was a great step-aerobics instructor and we had so much fun getting back into shape after having our babies. Along with other close friends, June had become a great support to me while our children grew and we discovered all of the issues my family would have to deal with regarding Travis' growth.

Mentally, Travis progressed fairly normal for his age, as far as we could tell, but there were definite challenges with regards to his physical development. Doctors at first told us Travis might not ever hold his head up. It took him eight months, but he did it. They also told us he probably wouldn't be able to sit on his own. It took him fifteen months, but he did that too. He began crawling on all fours at the age of seventeen months. Unfortunately, throughout this first year and a half, Travis was sick a lot as well. He spent many days in the hospital and was subjected to many medicines and treatments. We travelled to Edmonton often for his appointments at the Glennrose Hospital. The hospital and staff there were as curious of Travis' condition as they were supportive. Trisomy 9p is not well known and they were as eager to monitor and observe the changes in him as they were to help with his development.

Arlen and I met a few couples there every few weeks that would also have appointments for their children, and like us learning about the host of problems and issues. It was a curious thing to watch these couples, at first attending these appointments being loving, kind and supportive of each other, always attending the appointments together, but then eventually growing apart. We noticed that some even started to come by themselves. Later we found out, over several visits, that the pressure of raising a child with a disability was just too much for several of them and the couples eventually separated and many divorced. Arlen and I watched this happen and vowed, as we had on our wedding day, to support and love each other, whatever came our way. We were so fortunate to be able to always attend the appointments together. And by doing so, we were actively involved in knowing exactly what Travis needed by way of support from us, as well as with each other.

After a time, I began administering Ventolin (a medication to prevent bronchospasms) using a mask to help Travis breath. I found it to be quite a chore, considering I also had a two year old and a baby under a year old to look after. I would have to sit for about 15-20 minutes every four hours and just hold Travis while he breathed through the mask. Thankfully, Levi was such a great boy and would often sit with us. I would read to them and he would play while Devon napped or enjoyed the baby swing. Those times, which seemed to be such a burden to me then, are now some of my happiest memories.

Our life went on like this for months and we would have many days and even weeks, where Travis would do well even though the reflux in the back of his throat would still happen. We introduced solid foods to him eventually and, I tell you, it was nothing less than a horror the first time I saw solid food come out through his right nostril after he had swallowed a mouthful. We managed to pick foods that were easier for him to handle and he grew a little stronger.

As he aged, we began to see other effects of the Trisomy 9p. Travis' kidneys were delayed and so potty training was put on hold and he had a hernia to the right side of his belly button that would have to be monitored and eventually be taken care of. We noticed that his hearing wasn't very good and his eyesight even worse. We began giving him hearing tests to see how severe the hearing loss was and looked into the possibility of glasses to help with the vision loss.

Another physical abnormality, although they looked normal to the passing eye, was the creases of each of his fingers. They were not normal in the way that most people have two joints with creases above the base of each finger. These enable us to bend our fingers at those joints. You're looking at your fingers right now, aren't you? Travis' were just a little different, his fingers still bent in two places, but the length of the tip of his finger to the first joint or the first joint to the second, would be different on each finger, causing him to be able to bend his fingers in what looked to be odd places. They were double jointed and he used the ligaments to move his fingers rather than the muscle. They worked the same as yours and mine, but they looked almost comical sometimes.

Probably one of the biggest physical issues we were dealing with regarding Travis was his feet. His toes were recessed on the top of the pad of each foot, so it made it difficult to balance and walking was almost impossible. We were able to fit him with orthotic braces that strapped to his foot and extended up the back of his calves to his knee. Two straps wrapped around the brace and were held in place by Velcro. He was always upset that he had to wear industrial looking hiking boots instead of running shoes, but they were all we could find to fit around the width of the straps and brace.

So many times, at the end of the day, I would take his braces off and rub his poor little feet and legs. They would be a little red and often swollen where the straps fit across the top of his foot or the front of his shin. He would usually make his way to sit in our entry (where the family shoes were), trying on Levi's Batman runners and then trying to stand up in them. He loved those runners and I always felt bad we couldn't find him Batman boots.

After one particularly extreme case of pneumonia, a time when Travis was weaker than we had ever seen him, Arlen and I decided to do something that was (in my opinion) extreme; we took Travis to a chiropractor.

Arlen and his family had always believed in chiropractic care, but my family had always been terrified of being "cracked". The reason I eventually agreed to take Travis was because he was so, so sick and I was desperate to try anything. The other reason I made the decision, was because one of our best friends in high school, Larry Gingerrich, had become a chiropractor and I trusted him. The day we finally walked into the doctor's office, he looked up at us and said "I've been waiting for you to bring Travis to me."

Everything that Travis ate for that first 2 ½ years of his life, refluxed at the back of his throat and aspirated out through his nose. The first treatment Travis had with

Dr. Gingerrich was the very last time this happened. Honestly, miraculously, it stopped completely. Larry explained that because Travis was born so quickly, his neck, shoulders and nerves were severely compressed. One treatment and Travis had considerable relief and started to improve instantly.

A month later we returned to our specialists, who all (but one) were thrilled and wanted to learn more about the changes. One doctor was very narrow-minded and refused to believe that chiropractic care was even feasible for Travis' improvement. I send love, light and understanding to him, hoping that he has learned to become more open-minded since.

The doctors wanted to continue the drug regiments he was on, but eventually we also made a decision to stop all the medications he was on for reflux and the complications it caused. Our little man improved dramatically each day and the colds and sickness stopped completely. I have to say, without question, that I still believe in medical doctors and thank them every day for keeping our son alive while we figured out what all the issues were. However, the chiropractic adjustments were able to do for Travis what medicine couldn't. Although, we did still continue with medical care regarding Travis' other problems as well.

About eight months after that first Chiropractic appointment, I ran into one of the nurses who I had become friends with during Travis' extensive hospital stays. She made a remark that I hear replayed in my head often. She said, "it is so nice to see Travis looking so healthy; there was a time none of us nurses thought he would ever make it."

That day, I sat in my car and cried. I cried because I felt guilty for not realizing how sick my son was; I mean, I knew he was terribly sick, but I never, ever considered that he could have died. I just assumed that they would fix him. I just believed that they would be able to fix him.

Travis grew steadily stronger from then on and he was becoming such a character. He was determined to spend as much time hanging onto Levi as possible. Wherever Levi was, you could be sure that Travis was playing with him or vying for his attention. He would literally lie on poor Levi if he was watching TV or playing Nintendo. Levi was so good-natured, he would just gently move to a different spot and Travis would soon be sitting beside or laying on him again. Trav's hair was "poker straight", but a little wiry too and would often be standing up all over his head as each day progressed. Levi would often ask me to brush his hair, because it tickled his face when Trav was lying close to him.

The way Travis slept was also very unique. I recall arriving home one night after a hockey game out of town to a very flustered babysitter. She told me that things had gone really well and that the boys had played and gone to bed easily. However, an hour after she put them in their respective beds, she went to check on them and she freaked-out. She told us that when she looked into Travis' bed, she thought, "he was broken." I knew exactly what she meant and started to laugh. Travis would often sleep bent unusually far, backwards. The back of his head would almost touch the back of his feet. I don't know if it allowed him more air to breathe into his big barrel chest being bent in this position or if the double joints in his body allowed for the flexibility and it just felt good. I just know that it did look odd and I felt bad for the babysitter's distress.

One thing that was odd was that, although Travis was the one with many health issues, it was both Levi and Devon that I really had to watch when it came to colds and fevers.

Levi was the first to have a fever convulsion. I happened to be at an aerobics class when Arlen called to say he had to take Levi to the hospital. He had a high fever and had dropped to the floor with a convulsion.

A year later, I was at home and after putting the boys to bed, heard Devon's crib banging against the wall. I knew exactly what it was and ran up to see him having a convulsion. We were to learn that both boys were susceptible to these if their temperature spiked. We were cautious after that and only had one other incident.

Travis and Devon were very much alike at that time as far as their abilities were concerned. Because Travis' kidneys were also slow to develop, he wore a diaper for an extended period of time. He was also a bit smaller than he should have been because he had been sick so much, which made my two youngest appear to be about the same age.

I have a picture of the two of them, Travis and Devon, standing in our living room looking out the bay window, both wearing nothing but a diaper and they look as if they could be twins. In fact, many people who saw us, and didn't know us, thought they were twins.

By the time Levi was 5 years old, Travis 3 and Devon was 2, things were progressing well and continued to improve over the next couple of years. We had moved off the farm into town and Arlen began working for a trucking company as a driver and eventually became their dispatcher. I continued to work part time as a realtor and as a family; we enjoyed going to watch Arlen play hockey two or three times a week.

We continued to take Travis for chiropractic care and had regular visits to our family doctor and the team at the Glennrose regarding his hearing as well as to work on his other physical disabilities.

It was during one of the earlier visits to Edmonton and the team at the Glennrose Hospital, where my sister, pregnant with her first child, had agreed to accompany us to watch the boys while we were at Travis' appointment.

The hospital had a small shuttle bus that transported us to and from the hospital to our hotel. It was winter, around the end of February and on the return trip the shuttle bus slid sideways at an intersection and collided with another vehicle. Thank goodness Arlen was strong enough to be able to hold onto Travis while the driver did an extremely dangerous thing, considering the conditions of the roads. He slammed his breaks hard to stop at an intersection. This caused the bus to lurch forward, then moving sideways, and come to a stop against another vehicle in the lane beside it.

After spending time giving witness statements to a patrol officer called to the scene, we were all fine, tired and glad to arrive back at the hotel with nothing more than a frightening story to tell.

Eventually, Travis was progressing well and was able to go to an early playschool program where his world seemed to take off. He was shy the first few days and always wanted to be held, but after that, he jumped right into whatever activity the other kids were doing. He would concentrate very hard as he sat down to connect Lego pieces together because it was sometimes a bit difficult with his crooked little fingers. He would hurry over to join in at "circle time" and loved to move his arms and hands to the motion play games. His glasses were a bit of an issue at times as he would hide them or toss them into the play center or toy box. He always had a mischievous grin whenever you asked him where they were; he seemed to like the joke he was playing by hiding them.

One day, when I picked him up after class, one of his teachers told me that Travis' speech pathologist had asked them to make their voices go up and down rhythmically and to make different noises, but he would have none of that! He let her know that he wanted real words, not silly sounds that no one else was making. He seemed very self-aware and self-conscious of anything that set him apart from the other kids.

He continued to wear his braces, which kept his ankles stiff in place, and although some activities were difficult, like climbing and walking over uneven ground, he eventually learned to compensate and did quite well.

Whenever his class went on school outings, like to the park or the town library, an aid would pull a little hard plastic wagon for him to ride in, but most of the time, he would walk with the other children. He had a strong desire to always make sure the kids were ahead of him and would make a sound as if in reprimand to anyone who lagged behind the group. It was as if he was a duck gathering his ducklings ahead of him all the time, making sure they kept up with the group. We noticed that he always did this with Levi and Devon as well. Whenever we would go somewhere, Travis would walk behind the boys and make sure they were ahead of him. He would even push them forward or pinch them if he felt they needed a little encouragement. Often, he would get upset to the point of crying if he felt like someone was being left behind.

His need to keep his brothers ahead of him was most prevalent whenever we visited grandma and she put on his favorite animated movie, "Robin Hood". As the opening theme song by Roger Miller played,"Robin Hood and Little John walkin' through the forest, laughing back and forth at what the other one has to say; Reminiscing this and that and having such a good time, Oo-de-laly, oo-de-lally, golly, what a day…" all three boys would jump up and march around the coffee table. Levi would lead the parade, Devon would follow and as always, Travis would bring up the rear, pushing his brothers ahead of him, laughing while he marched, knees high in the air. He loved every minute of that song and we laughed every time at their enthusiasm.

Another love of Travis' was water. He often played in the water table activity center at school and bath time was always a favorite activity. It was never a chore to get him into the tub but rather, it was always a chore to get him out.Arlen's mom would often take him to one of our little community pools and he was always upset when it was time to leave. I believe that the water felt good on his feet and I also think that he enjoyed it because he didn't have to wear his braces for that activity, yet his feet were under water, so he didn't feel like anyone was looking at them.

He was shy with new kids upon first meeting them, often observing them for a long while before interacting with them, but didn't seem to be as shy with adults. He was curious about other kids and eventually mimicked their play. I was so fortunate to be given written reports, daily, of all the things Travis did because he was enrolled in a grant program through the government and the local school division. This program was such a blessing because it allowed us extra time in the evening as a family, to just enjoy each other, knowing that he was working hard every day on his developmental skills. The interaction between his aids and us made for a very successful learning environment.

Then it came time for him to be enrolled into kindergarten. We were assigned a personal aid, also through a government program, to help with Travis' development; her name was Shawna. She was wonderful and became a very important person in Travis' life, and of course, in our lives as well. She was his best buddy and, although he often let her know when he didn't want to do something, they got along perfectly and we love her. We especially love her gentle character and were so thankful for her capacity to work with all of us, to help assist and improve his everyday life. Shawna would often babysit all three of our boys when we needed her outside of school hours as well.

It was during that first year of kindergarten for Travis, that Devon started CanSkate, a beginner skating program. Levi had started playing hockey the year before and Travis loved to go with me to their practices. His feet were impossible to put into skates which meant he couldn't participate, so he would walk along the stands, banging on the glass and laugh when his brothers fell or he would cheer them on as they skated by.

Like many kids at the rink, Travis especially loved to watch the Zamboni clean the ice. His favorite driver was an older gentleman who wore a cowboy hat. Travis would stand watching as the machine made its way around and around the ice. Then when the driver waved at him, he would laugh. His laughter was so infectious and would often cause others to laugh with him.

His rink family treated him like any other, normal little boy and I loved to take him there. When we would get home from the rink, Travis could almost always be found in our little front entry, trying on his brother's skates and trying his best to stand up.

Although having tubes implanted in his ears had helped greatly with his hearing, there was still enough hearing loss to inhibit Travis' speech. I will never forget the first time I heard him address me; he would not just say "mama", but would always say, "mum mum mum mum mum". He would say, "da da" for Arlen and he had little sounds he made for his brothers. After a time, he was able to say "Pooh" for "Winny the Pooh" and "horse".

We had all learned some basic sign-language to communicate, but we never really had a problem knowing what Travis wanted. His needs were simple, and he was always able to let us know by a look or a sound exactly what he wanted. And it was clear, he wanted to wear those skates.

People often told me that they wished they knew what he was thinking because he seemed to be such an old soul for someone so young. He seemed to say so much with a look or a sound that was incoherent to us.

CHAPTER 4

Shriners, Blue Angels and Batman Shoes

During the summer of 1998, we rented a small lot at a private camp ground on the shores of Lesser Slave Lake and we enjoyed spending time camping with friends and family. On one beautiful weekend, Levi invited his best buddy Brook to camp with us.

Arlen and I spent our time getting the lot in shape; mowing, trimming and removing overgrown trees and shrubs. To keep the boys busy and out of the way while we worked, we let them take the ATV quad for a ride. The boys were having a great time riding it around in first gear on our big grass lawn in front of the lake. All four of them could sit one behind the other and putt-putt around and around.

We hadn't heard about it until later, that one of the owners of the campground approached the boys to tell them to get off the grass. Since we had already seen other quads do the same, we had no idea they weren't allowed to be there. The boys decided to take the little ring road around to the back of our camp instead of taking the direct, flat route over the lawn.

Unfortunately, they drove too close to the edge of the path and the quad tipped over onto its side. Levi, Devon and Travis jumped free of the big machine, but Brook was stuck underneath the weight of it and hot oil dripped out of the engine onto his leg before we could lift it off of him.

Our other two boys were fine, but Travis must have banged his nose, because it became quite swollen. We took Brook to the emergency room where I received quite a lecture about the dangers of quads from the nurse. She proceeded to tell me how horseback riding was a much better activity for people.

Later in the waiting room I recall looking at a magazine cover and seeing a picture of Christopher Reeve in a wheelchair. I remember thinking, how ironic is that? Superman was thrown from a horse.

The emergency staff bandaged-up Brook and since his parents (who are distant relatives) were out of town, we kept him with us over night; he was such a little trooper.

Unfortunately, a short time later, it was apparent that Brook would need skin grafts to repair the scaring on his leg. Luckily, Brooks' great uncle was a member of the Shriners organization and they arranged to have him treated by the doctors in Sacramento, California where the Shriners Hospital for Children specializes in bones and burns.

When they met with the doctors to come up with a plan for Brook's care, his family thankfully thought of Travis and the problem with his feet. Wanda, Brook's mom, called me after they returned from their first visit to the Shriners hospital and brought application papers to me. After we filled out the Shriners application, we were told that they would love to see what they could do for us. We were thrilled.

That year, the year Travis turned five, Arlen and I travelled to Sacramento to meet a team of doctors to come up with a care plan. The Shriners paid for the flight for Travis and one parent, and we managed to come up with enough to pay for the extra ticket so we could both go. It was an amazing trip. We met wonderful people and stayed for 4 days.

Because his appointments were done early the second day, we actually had an extra day to spend sightseeing. So, we decided to rent a car and drive to San Francisco. The rental car was a big, old Mercury Grand Marquis and it felt like we were driving a boat. Travis sat between us in the wide front seat and laughed and laughed when Arlen drove a little too fast over the swells and bumps going down the steep hills.

In San Francisco, we took a ride on the trolley, which also thrilled Travis into giggles. Later on, we all spent a day in the sun looking around Fisherman's Wharf and ate at Bubba Gump's restaurant.

It was after a fantastic meal and enjoying our dessert that we suddenly felt the restaurant shudder. At first we panicked, thinking it was an earthquake, but were surprised when a Blue Angel fighter jet, standing on end, floated by the windows of the restaurant in the bay!

After questioning one of the waiters of the restaurant, we found out that there was an air show scheduled for the next morning. It didn't take but a shared look across the table for Arlen and me to decide we wanted to see that show. We promptly crossed the street and found a hotel for the night. We weren't missing this for anything!

We were fortunate enough to find a room at the hotel but it only had one bed for all three of us. Although it was a king size, I remember waking up early the next morning to find Travis sprawled crossways, his head resting against Arlen's shoulder and his feet laying across my stomach. Both Arlen and I were pushed to the edge of each of our side of the bed and Travis was spread out, thoroughly enjoying the rest of the bed. When I woke him, tickling the bottom of his feet, he giggled and snuggled in deeper.

The next day, Travis was very excited as we watched the jet planes. I'm sure he could feel the intense vibrations from the power. He loved it when people put coins down on the dock so when the jets flew-by, the force would make the coins jump and bounce all over. He laughed and stamped his feet and pointed at the coins as they danced all over the surface of the dock. Even thought it was a crazy, busy trip back to Sacramento in the insane weekend traffic (the likes of which we had never seen) the air show made it well worth it. The trip home the next day was uneventful and we looked forward to hearing from the hospital regarding his continued care.

We didn't have to wait long. A few weeks later, in October of 1998, I travelled back and stayed in the hospital for 12 days with my little man where they were to do the surgery to correct his feet. Arlen was not able to accompany us on this trip as the Shriners only paid for Travis and one parent and we were unable to afford the extra ticket or pay for 12 days in a hotel. I was told I would be able to sleep on a cot in Travis' room at the hospital.

When we arrived at the airport in Sacramento, a Shriner met us and drove us to the hotel where we stayed for that first night. We were shown to our room, which was on the first floor, and after a quick supper of crackers and an apple from the vending machine, we settled down to get some sleep.

It had been a long and exhausting day. We had to fly from Edmonton to Seattle, to Portland and then on to Sacramento. I awoke a few hours later, to the sound of rain banging hard against the window. So, I got up to look out at the small empty swimming pool outside our window. As I looked at the rain splashing down into it, I was a little disappointed that it wasn't a couple months earlier since I knew Travis would have loved to be in the water. I stood there for a moment pondering the days ahead before heading to the washroom and going back to bed.

As I flipped the switch in the small hotel bathroom, I had to stop myself from screaming and waking Travis. I looked at the floor where a thousand small black bugs were crawling all over the tile floor. I was horrified! I grabbed the only thing I had handy, my hairspray, and I sprayed the heck out of them.

I hopped back into the nice bug-free bed. However, there were so many and it freaked me out enough that I sat up until morning, watching my little boy sleep and keeping an eye out for crawlies.

By morning, there was not a trace of the critters anywhere and when I mentioned the incident to the front desk clerk, she didn't seem surprised or concerned at all. She told me that this was a regular occurrence every time it rained. I made a mental note to ask for an upper floor when we would be returning to the same hotel for our trip home.

After another meal from the vending machines, because there didn't appear to be a restaurant close, we were picked up by a Shriner and taken to the hospital. Once we had signed in, we were greeted by a man in a friendly looking clown costume and then shown, along with a few others, to the family lounge.

A Shriner stayed with us to answer any questions and help us in any way, and after a time a social worker came in and held an informal introduction and question period. Then we were taken on a tour of some areas of the hospital. We saw the operating and recovery room, parent apartments and the social services area; as well as the cafeteria, recreation and play therapy areas. After that we were shown to our rooms and made comfortable.

Our situation was a bit unique; since Travis was older, he was not put into a constantly monitored crib-room, yet, due to his delayed abilities he couldn't be left unattended either. I was given a room in the parent apartments, but because of Travis' inability to communicate; I ended up sleeping in a big chair in his room, in case he needed me. I only used the apartment to shower and change when the nurses had time to stay with him.

We weren't there for very long before another "fuzzy hat" (as we liked to call the Shriners), came to our room with gifts for the patients. Travis was given a little hard paper book, a wooden car and a quilted red and white striped lap blanket. We were to find out that this gift giving was something that took place almost every day at this hospital. My luggage was going to be full on the way home.

The next morning, which was a Thursday, we were scheduled to go to a surgical conference. We were shown to a room set up much like a theater where 20 or more doctors and specialists were seated. They started out by asking our social worker some medical questions regarding Travis since she had all the information from his previous hospital visits. They then asked me about the history of his medical issues and went on to watch as I held his hand and walked back and forth with him with and without his braces on so they could see how his feet and legs worked.

Travis did very well, but he cried a bit when I took his boots and braces off and made him walk barefoot across the front of the crowd. He loved to walk barefoot at home, where he was comfortable with family and our friends seeing him, but he didn't want these strangers seeing his poor little feet. Although he was born with his feet that way and it wasn't a result of an accident or incident, Travis knew his feet were different than anyone else's and didn't like attention drawn to them.

After a few rounds back and forth, we were then asked to wait outside for a moment while they went over his x-rays and other medical charts. A representative came out about 45 minutes later and told us their plan of action. Travis was to have 2 pins put in his left foot and one in his right. They were going to reposition his toes and do a partial infusion of the bone. They planned to also take a piece of bone from his hip and make a "stopper" of sorts in his feet as well as do a tendon lengthening or release as needed.

I felt a little sick to my stomach as this news was given to me. I imagined the pain Travis would have to endure and felt so sorry for our little man, even though I knew it was eventually going to make him very happy to have his feet fixed. He would be in casts for six weeks and then we would return to have them checked and replaced for another six weeks. From there, he would wear braces again for three months and after that, he would be able to walk like anyone else without the use of support. I held onto an image of his smiling face when he would finally be able to walk with normal running shoes, took a deep breath and made up my mind to be strong for him. The surgery time was set for the following Monday and so, we waited.

Travis and I met so many wonderful people at the hospital and I was amazed by the amount of love and respect given to each and every patient. There was one special teenage girl named Annie who was so wonderful with Travis. She was in the hospital for some minor reconstructive foot surgery. He couldn't talk and he couldn't hear, yet they became fast friends. Since she was in the hospital for bone related issues as well, I would take Travis to her room so he could snuggle up with her on her bed while she read to him or played with his toys. Even though we were still learning a bit of sign language, Travis could communicate very well regardless and the two of them didn't seem to have any issue getting along.

The environment of the hospital is one I will never forget. I saw children fighting through horribly painful situations with smiles on their faces, while their parents seemed on the edge of breaking. I remember one little boy, sitting in the playroom trying to play Nintendo. The tips of several of his fingers had been burned off in an accident, but had been repaired as best they could and they were healing. His mother sat beside her son, watching him maneuver the controls with his sore little hands; she was quietly sobbing. The little boy just wanted to play the game, and was concentrating so hard on how to make the controls work, his way. I don't think he even realized the impact his accident would have on his life, but the mom did and as I made eye contact with her, we shared a moment of understanding that only parents watching their children endure would recognize.

We happened to be there at the end of October and the hospital staff came to our room with a dinosaur costume for Travis because they were going to have a pre-Halloween party on the Saturday night. He looked adorable in the little blue suit with big polka dots and long tail. After getting him dressed up, we were led to an area of the hospital where we could knock on special, decorated doors. Each door would open and someone with a smiling face would give candy to the kids as they held open the bags that were supplied to them and said "trick or treat". Travis even tried to mimic me when I said it for him and my heart swelled. By the time we had gone to each door, a nurse met us and handed Travis a Certificate of Achievement for the "Cutest Dinosaur". There was so much happiness that day.

The night before the surgery, a man who happened to be in a wheelchair came to visit us. His job at the hospital, being a play therapist, was to go to each of the children before their surgery and show them some of the things they might see in the operating room so they wouldn't be quite so frightened. We laughed as this man put a surgeon's cap on Trav's head, put a gown on him and blew up a rubber glove. I thought it was genius of the hospital to do this simple act of pure kindness for the children. I am sure Travis didn't understand the reasoning behind all the stuff he was being introduced to and allowed to play with, but it certainly was fun and made me feel good.

The day came for his surgery and I have never felt so alone in my life. The hospital staff was so wonderful and the surgeons, anesthesiologists, nurses and even the cast crew came out to greet us and to tell me that they would take great care of Travis. My heart broke as my son was wheeled away, arms stretched out to me, eyes questioning as to why I would let him go with these strangers, a look that begged me to pick him up, and scared because he didn't know what was going on.

As I saw him being pushed further down the hall, crying and struggling to turn around to see me, I stood in the hallway and I cried. I cried and I wondered if Travis was going to be angry with me when he saw me next. I was so sad that he had to go through something that would bring him more pain and I cried, fearing that something might go wrong.

All at once, an amazing calm came over me and I knew what I had to do. In the middle of this place, where success comes out of so much pain and hard work, I dropped to my knees, folded my fingers together, closed my eyes and I prayed. I prayed for my son, I prayed for the people working on him, I prayed for the people who brought us to this point and I prayed that I would have enough strength to handle what was to come.

A moment later, as I opened my eyes, with renewed faith and a greater sense of peace, I was humbled to see a dozen or more people, on their knees, praying right along beside me. I could barely make it to my feet as the tears blurred my eyes, but many hands reached forward to help. A moment or two of hugs and well wishes passed and then all those wonderful people went about their day. I will always remember their kindness and I will always remember the day, when for the very first time in my life, I really prayed.

Travis was gone for more than two hours and it was the longest two hours ever. Back then we didn't have cell phones and Facebook, so communication and sharing comfort with Arlen back home was not very easy. In the waiting room, however, volunteers sat with the parents waiting for their children having surgery that day. They brought coffee or tea to whoever wanted it and were there offering comfort and support. I was on my own, but I no longer felt quite so alone.

I was so happy and relieved when they called me to recovery, but it nearly broke my heart to see Travis in so much pain. He had always been such a tough little guy and had never really showed much pain, but we knew he must have often been in a great deal of discomfort. That day, however, I saw real pain. Every time I tried to lift his blankets to look at the casts on his feet or the bandage at his hip, he would cry and try to cover them back up. I don't know if he didn't want me to see the casts or if he just didn't want to see them himself.

Recovery began and I didn't leave his room; I watched him sleep and when he awoke, often crying, I hugged him and hummed "Greensleeves" to comfort him; or perhaps it was to comfort me.

A couple of days later, rather than using a wheelchair, I was given a little red plastic wagon lined with pillows to set Travis in. I was then able to pull him around and get him out of his bed (and both of us out of that room).

Travis loved this idea and I was amazed by other fantastic ideas facilitated by the hospital as well. There were toy rooms and games set up for the patients as well as a library, which was especially handy for me. I read "The Diary of Ann Frank" while Travis slept and recovered.

Before we left the hospital a few days later, Travis was given his greatest gift; a pair of long, wide knitted socks that covered over his casts. They were brightly colored and he was happy to wear them.

The trip home was not fun. I had abandoned my umbrella stroller at the hospital in trade for a wheelchair to help transport Travis home and had to take several pillows with me and prop them around him as the wheelchair was an adult chair and much too big for him.

The night before we flew home, we stayed in the same hotel where we had on our arrival stay. It was near the airport and our flight was early the next day. Remembering the frightful little bug experience from the first journey, I requested to not have a ground floor room. Luckily, I was only given one on the second floor because I hadn't noticed that there weren't any elevators in this hotel. So, it was quite a chore to get us and our luggage up to the room considering Trav was in a wheelchair. I carried him up first and laid him on the bed, returned for the chair and then returned for our luggage. It was exhausting.

The first part of the next day's journey went fairly well, our flights went from Sacramento to Idaho, to Seattle and then on to Edmonton. However, before we could land in Edmonton, the pilot came over the speaker system announcing that a storm in the city made it impossible for us to land and we were being rerouted to Calgary.

Once in Calgary, we found out they had arranged a bus to pick us up to travel the 3 hours to Edmonton by ground. I was tired and frustrated, feeling so very sorry for Travis and the pain he was in.

Approximately an hour into the trip, wind from the storm managed to grab one of the vents at the top of the passenger bus (about 4 rows ahead of us) forcing it open. One of the taller, male passengers jumped up and grabbed it, holding it in place, so that it wouldn't completely fly off. He was standing there with another man who was trying to figure out a way to secure it, when the bus suddenly swerved aggressively to the right and drove down into the ditch. The two of us were sitting in the very back seat, which sat 3 across giving us room for Travis to lie down and, with the aid of some pain medication, he had managed to fall asleep. Thankfully, I was able to hold him securely as the bus came to a stop and he didn't wake up.

Apparently, an accident a few car lengths ahead of us caused a domino effect of sudden stops in our lane. Our bus driver couldn't stop in time to avoid an accident, so he chose to take to the ditch. The banks were not steep and he skillfully managed to keep it on its wheels, coming to a fairly slow, somewhat gentle stop.

After a time, everyone settled down and we all caught our breath; the two men secured the vent and the traffic started again. The driver maneuvered the bus gently out of the ditch and we made our way slowly to Edmonton in the continuing storm.

I was never so happy to see my silver minivan (and eventually the hotel near the airport) as I was that night. Travis and I had a great sleep and headed home in sunny skies the next day.

Our third trip was scheduled 6 weeks later for a check-up and to change Travis' casts. Since Brook had to return to the hospital for his appointment as well, Wanda, Brook, Travis and I all travelled together. We stayed at the Ronald McDonald house near the hospital, which was a fantastic facility and after having successful appointments, had a wonderfully uneventful trip home.

It took a few months of recovery, and another trip to the hospital, but "Our Little Man" was finally able to take the casts off and be fitted back into braces.

Once again, we had extra time on this last visit to the Shriners, giving Travis and I the opportunity to visit a small mall near the hospital. He now wore braces, so I decided to use a cart available for mall patrons and I put him into it.

He was facing me with his legs dangling out through the openings in the front. We strolled along, looking at decorated windows and I stopped outside one store to flip through a rack of clothes. Trav was sitting in the cart and as I made my way around the rack. Suddenly I heard an odd noise, like Travis giving someone heck. I turned just in time to see a young man pushing the cart Travis was in, down the mall hallway, away from me!

It took only a moment for me to register what was happening and I chased after them. The boy was running wildly down the hall, trying to lift Travis out of the cart. My heart was racing in my chest and I felt like I couldn't breathe; in my head, I was screaming, but not a sound came out of my mouth; I was terrified. Ironically, the braces on his feet (the very ones that we both loved to hate) made it (thankfully) incredibly difficult for the boy to pull him out easily.

He kept lifting up on him, but the inability for Trav's legs to bend at the ankle, and the length of hard plastic, kept him from being able to pull him free from the cart.

It was then that I noticed a mall security guard come out from behind an escalator entrance and the boy panicked, pushing the cart away from him. The guard was able to stop the young man and thankfully, Travis wasn't hurt and the cart had remained on its wheels.

I grabbed Travis and hugged him until my heart slowed down. Only then was I able to carefully take him out of the cart. I stood there hugging him while he cried and pointed to the boy being placed in handcuffs. He seemed to be giving the boy a stern reprimand and eventually it actually made me giggle, probably from nerves. My strong little man!

In all the action, I hadn't even noticed that there was another mall security guard running a couple steps behind me. Apparently, the boy had been spotted shoplifting and when the guard approached him, he ran. He must have panicked and decided to use Travis to get away. Thank God he was unable to get Travis extricated from the cart or things could have ended quite differently.

After calming everyone down, the boy was led away and I was led to a room to make a statement. My biggest concern was for Travis, but he seemed to settle easily and as I was exhausted, we returned to the hospital and rested until the next morning when we were to leave.

Three months later, Travis was given the go ahead to remove the braces and we were able to buy him his first pair of running shoes.

It was during this time when I first felt compelled to find a church to attend where I could give thanks. I just felt the need and I decided to go to the local Baptist church since I knew a few people who attended there. It wasn't a big church like the one I had already been to a few times with my aunt and uncle; it was a small congregation and I was drawn to go there.

The first day I went by myself, I snuck into the back row after the service started and I sat for a few minutes on the smooth, hard wooden pew before I started to cry. I don't know why, but such a deep feeling of relief spread over me as well as an incredible sense of peace.

A lady that I don't know came to the back, sat beside me and just held my hand throughout the service. I thanked her for her kindness and left immediately afterward.

I returned the next week, as well as the week after. Eventually, I took my family and we attended regularly after that. It was wonderful to be part of a church community.And even though we met and became friends with many people over the next year, it always puzzled me that I never saw that lady again after that first day, but I will never forget her thoughtfulness.

By the next summer, Travis continued to improve greatly. He had become such a little man. He wore his glasses more consistently so he could see better. We were still working on the sign language skills while attending clinics to figure out what to do about his slight hearing loss, although the tubes implanted in his ears helped a great deal. We also continued to monitor his kidney issues.

Following the surgery, his legs had improved so much so that he woke up every morning and, after getting dressed, would choose Levi's Batman running shoes, which now fit him perfectly, or cowboy boots to wear to school. Both of these he wore with great pride.

My mother and her sister owned a bakery and coffee shop in our little town and we would often stop in to visit. Most days, Travis would peer over the cooler into the display where tubs of ice cream sat beneath the glass. He would point to whatever tub he decided held the type of ice cream he would have that day.

My mom recalls the first day Travis walked in without his braces, sporting just his runners and sat down at a table instead of heading straight to the cooler. He motioned for grandma to come over and proceeded to lift his foot up. Then pointing at his shoes and then at Levi's shoes; he wanted grandma to recognize that he was wearing shoes just like his big brother. My heart melted and grandma had a tear in her eye.

Travis' footwear was so important to him. In fact, even when he wore shorts or his swim trunks, he would wear his sneakers or cowboy boots. I found a pair of rubber boots, which he approved of, that he could easily slip on and off. These were his fashion statement that summer.

Weekends spent at the lake that summer were such fun. During the days the boys would fish and play in the water, wading through the weeds to catch frogs. Then at night we would sit around the campfire, snuggled under blankets.

One particular trip toward the end of that June ended in a not so pleasant memory; however, looking back on it, I can laugh now. We had packed everyone into our van, tired and in need of baths and started the 20 km drive home Sunday night, when Travis started to fuss. This was not like him at all, he was generally happy most of the time, he certainly did not whine like that. Then it hit me, about the same time as Travis threw up all over the floor. We had fed the boys hotdogs over the fire just a couple of hours before leaving the camp. I was busy packing everything up for the trek home while Arlen got the fire going. When the coals were hot enough for cooking, he handed Levi and Devon their own sticks to cook their hotdogs while Arlen cooked two on his; one for him and one for Travis. I came out of the camper to see Travis over at the table we had set up outside, he had a raw hotdog in his hand and a rather large mouthful of another. He was hungry and apparently couldn't wait for a cooked hotdog.

I thought that he had only eaten one raw hotdog, but the sheer magnitude of what now pooled all over the floor of the van suggested otherwise. It took Arlen about three seconds to pull the van over to the side of the road and open the sliding side door.

Both Levi and Devon, who could get themselves out of their seatbelts, along with Arlen and I, bailed, leaving poor Travis to sit alone in the van. It smelled awful and the four of us stood in the ditch gagging and arguing over who was going to clean it up.

All of a sudden, we heard Travis laughing hysterically. There he sat, still strapped into his booster seat, apparently feeling much better, pointing and laughing at us. I imagine it did look pretty funny to anyone passing by. Eventually, we decided as a family (my boys knew better than to side against their mom) that Arlen would clean it up.

Travis' progress was remarkable and the freedom of movement he had now that he was out of the leg braces was incredible. By the first week of August, things were going extremely well. My niece was having a birthday party and had decided; since it was so hot out, to set up a portable swimming pool in her back yard. Each of the kids at the party took turns standing at the hand held pump to pump up the little plastic pool. When it came time for Travis to take a turn, he stood there with a giggle and the biggest smile on his face while he pulled the pump up and pushed it down. We all saw the pride he felt in being able to do what the other kids could do.

CHAPTER 5

Those Words

oward the end of that same summer of 1999, some very good friends of ours, Mel and Tracy, decided to come to spend the weekend camping with us at our lake lot. They had 3 children at the time and because they lived in a town just over an hour away, we thought it would be nice to visit before the kids all went back to school in September. Levi would be headed to grade three, Travis grade one and Devon would be just starting kindergarten.

After a busy and fun couple of days playing baseball and swimming, eating and enjoying the noisy chatter of six kids around the campfire, we awoke Sunday morning to find the day was kind of cool and dreary. After a large breakfast of pancakes and bacon, a couple of the kids wanted to go swimming, but we decided it was safer for them to head down along the waterfront toward the marina so they could fish instead.

While we were there, Eric, Mel and Tracy's oldest son, who had been diagnosed with cerebral palsy, had a slight seizure and fell on the ramp where the boats are loaded in and out of the water. He had bumped his head pretty hard when he fell and would definitely need stitches. I immediately ran back to our site to get our van so I could drive it around to the marina entrance.

When I got there, they had already cleaned the wound a bit and put a compression bandage on it to slow the bleeding. We loaded Eric and his mom, Tracy, into the van and I walked around to get into the driver's seat to drive the 20 km into town and to our local hospital.

As I came around the front of the van, I saw that Travis was standing with his hand against the driver's door. So, I picked him up and gave him a quick hug; he giggled in my ear, so I kissed him on the nose before I handed him to Arlen. I smiled at them because Arlen was tickling him as I drove away.

While we sat at the hospital, waiting for the doctor on-call to come and stitch the cut on Eric's head, the nurse came into the trauma room and told us that she would have to move us to a secondary room as they had an emergency coming in that would take priority. She said there had been an accident at Joussard, the little hamlet where our lake lot was, and they were bringing someone in.

I remember sitting down, hard, in a chair and saying to the nurse, "It's Travis". Both Tracy and the nurse looked at me like I was a little bit crazy as the nurse said she didn't know details or even if it was a child or an adult, but I knew. I felt it.

A few minutes later, that same nurse came to tell us that it was Travis that was being brought in and that he had been run over by a vehicle. Tracy sat with me and we prayed while we waited. When I heard the ambulance siren screaming as it turned into the hospital parking lot, I ran to the Emergency entrance doors.

It seemed to take forever for the automatic doors of the hospital to open as I peered through to the ambulance backing into place; I was just stepping through when the big double back doors opened. Arlen jumped down and out of the way as the attendants pulled the stretcher free, that's when I first saw my little man strapped to the stretcher. He was unconscious and looked so very pale, but I could see the shallow rise and fall of his chest, so I took a deep breath; I hadn't even realized that I had been holding it. I noticed his torn shirt and the dirt streaked across part of his cheek and his face and head looked swollen. I looked at Arlen and asked, "Who did it?" He looked up at me with so much pain and panic in his eyes as he said "June." I know there are people that don't believe me, but at that moment, I have to tell you, I felt nothing but a huge amount of relief wash over me. Let me explain why.

There were people who, at that time, had a lot near ours. They spent quite a bit of time drinking and driving from their campsite to another friend's campsite. I was relieved that it was not them, because it crossed my mind that I probably would not have been able to forgive them for drinking and driving. I also felt extremely relieved that it was not Arlen. I knew that June loved Travis. I knew that she would not have done anything remotely close to this on purpose. I knew it was an accident, plain and terribly simple. It was an accident and I wouldn't have to deal with blaming anyone for it.

Apparently, after I left, Barry and June had showed up at the lake with a new shed to be placed at the lot they had just rented a little ways from ours. Arlen, Mel and the kids all went over to say, "hi" and help where they could. June's vehicle was in the way of where they wanted to put the shed, so she jumped in to move it. She didn't realize that Travis was standing at her back bumper and she backed over the length of him. The vehicle pushed him over and the rear driver's side tire ran him over from feet to head.

Arlen recalls hearing a "thud" and turned around to see the vehicle parked on top of Travis. June felt the impact and realizing she had hit something, put the vehicle into drive and moved ahead off of him. Arlen and Barry immediately ran to assess the situation and started first aid. At this point June was hysterical and stood beside them as they worked on him. She kept frantically saying, "I'm so sorry, I'm so sorry, I didn't see him."

It seemed to take forever for the ambulance to arrive; we later learned they had gotten lost. Once they loaded Travis into the ambulance, Arlen rode with them as they made their way to the main highway. There was a moment when Arlen argued with the EMTs to go to the High Prairie emergency since it was closer, while the Ambulance attendants thought Slave Lake emergency was closer.

Arlen said he was also frustrated at the Ambulance driver when he pulled over for seemingly no apparent reason to the side of the road en route to the hospital. However, they did this so the Paramedic could meet them along the way, as the ambulance attendants were not qualified to handle this type of crisis.

They rushed Travis through the doors, down the short hallway, around the corner and into the trauma room of the emergency center while we followed behind. So many family and friends started to arrive. I don't remember who was all there, but I remember looking into everyone's panicked and sorrow filled eyes as they arrived. I do recall a bit when June arrived, because there was just a little more confusion and noise. I just sat while everyone told me he would be okay. My heart pounded, the tears flowed, I prayed and we waited.

The doctor on-call that day happened to be a real estate client of mine. He was new to town and I had just finished helping his family purchase a house. When he came out of the trauma room, the noise stopped and I could hear the blood pounding in my head. As he moved toward Arlen and me, everything slowed down; you could sense that it was not going to be good news. People started to gather close from the lobby and surrounding rooms near the ER.

Dr. Vu had only recently moved to Canada and his English was not very good and as he stood in front of us with all of our family and friends surrounding us he awkwardly said "I'm sorry, he dead".

I will forever hear those words in my head.

Immediately, I heard June scream, "No, No Diane, he can't be, Arlen?" People started crying. I grabbed June and hugged her while I reached for Arlen, who hugged us both. I was stunned. My head was spinning. I looked around and vaguely remember people talking to me, but I couldn't focus, I could barely keep my feet under me. My legs felt like they were made of rubber, but it didn't matter, I was numb. I felt as if everything was going a hundred miles an hour, but I was just standing there watching it go by.

After a few moments (or a long while, I don't remember), we were led into the trauma room where Travis lay. He still had a tube stuck down his throat that was taped to and ran into his nose and he was badly swollen around the head and face. Arlen's parents were in the room and so was my mom. Arlen was knelt down at the head of the bed, sobbing loudly while he stroked Travis' hair and I stood at the side of the bed, crying while I rubbed my hands down his arm then held and kissed his crooked little fingers.

I remember thinking that I wanted everyone to leave, to get away from my beautiful little boy, so that I could clean him up and change his clothes. We stood there, crying that way for what seemed like a very long time; now it seems like it wasn't nearly long enough.

All of a sudden, I was given the greatest gift anyone could receive in the face of such a tragedy. I saw or felt or sensed Travis' energy as it lifted, floating from his broken little body and rise to the corner of the room. I looked up to my right as it hovered for the briefest moment in the corner, as if to say "goodbye" and then, gently, quietly, it simply left; virtually dissipating in the air.

A great calm came over me at that moment and I managed to maneuver my way backwards to sit in a chair that leaned against the wall in the room. I sat there, quietly observing and trying to make sense of everything that had just happened. It was weeks later that Arlen's dad asked me what happened in the room that day, as he had noticed the sudden change in me and was curious. That's when I shared with them what I had witnessed. What I had been blessed with that day.

From that moment on, I was able to comprehend the difference between the physical body and the energy of our soul. I thank God for that gift.

As we moved out of the room some time later, leaving the precious body of my son for the hospital staff to look after, I remember Tracy hugging me and saying "My heart is breaking for you". My heart was definitely broken, clean through.

After people started to leave, I recall looking over at a friend of mine who was in her RCMP uniform. She led us to a room where she gave her condolences and then spoke to us about organ donation. We had to tell her we didn't think it was an option because of his genetic disorder and she said she understood, but was required to ask.

I don't remember at all leaving the hospital or how I got home. Our house was close; in fact, we could see it from the back entrance of the hospital, not even a block away. I found out years later that everyone left and my mother was forgotten at the hospital. She had to walk to our house by herself and that saddens me. My father was at home at the time and met us at the house later.

CHAPTER 6

The Blur and the Angel Club

The days that followed Travis' accident are somewhat of a blur. We had to first and foremost go home and tell our sons, Levi who had just turned 8 and Devon, who was 5, that their beautiful brother would not be coming home, ever. There were tears and there were questions and there was an awful lot of stunned silence.

Cards, letters, flowers, plants, food and more food arrived daily. People were everywhere. Arlen and I both come from large families, so there were always at least 20 or more people in our house, on our deck and hanging out on the front lawn. Mel and Tracy actually set up their camper in our backyard to be near us until after the funeral.

The day after the accident was spent just trying to figure out what needed to be done. Thankfully, family and friends jumped in and helped out. That morning, I realized that Trav's glasses were nowhere to be found and I felt panicked about it for some strange reason. I knew they had not been taken to the hospital and I wondered where they were. A family friend, Byron, took the time to go back out to the lake lot to look around.

He found the glasses lying in some tall grass beside our camper where we had loaded everyone in the back of a pickup the morning of the accident to head down to the marina. Was that only just the day before? It gave me great comfort to have those glasses to hang onto, knowing they were such a big part of him. It was also on that day that someone made an appointment with the funeral director for the following morning.

That afternoon, I decided to go to my room and rest for a few minutes. I needed to get away from everyone and I suddenly felt a need to put on paper, a written good bye to my son. The words flowed from me as if they came from somewhere else and we chose to put those words in his funeral card.

> *Our Little Man was sent here by God*
> *To touch so many with his selfless love*
> *He taught those around him to live for that day*
> *Now he's running and jumping in heaven, we pray*
> *He's asking the Lord all the questions he can*
> *Those questions we tried, but could not understand*
> *Be brave my boy, the pain is forgotten*
> *Our love is strong; we'll not forget what you taught us*
> *Have fun and go play, we'll see you another day*
> *And we know on that day, when our time has come*
> *You'll be standing at the gates to usher us home.*
> *Love Mom*

When we met the funeral director, it all seemed surreal to me. Picking the final resting place for your son is not the way it is supposed to be! Deciding on pallbearers and honorary pallbearers for a six year old is a task I don't wish for anyone. Choosing which picture to use for the funeral card and which casket to lay his handsome body in, is something no parent should ever have to do.

We decided to ask Shawna, his aid at school, to help us finalize the list of honorary pallbearers, since she knew better which kids he played with while at school. We also asked her to do the eulogy. When they asked us to pick flowers for the top of the casket, we chose stargazer lilies. My boys had bought me a bouquet of them just 10 days before the accident to celebrate Arlen and my 10th wedding anniversary.

When we were asked to pick songs to play at the funeral, besides some traditional hymns, we decided to use a song that Arlen had noticed Travis dancing to in front of the T.V. just a few days before. Even though he was partially deaf, something about the video and vibrations of this particular song captivated him. He would come running from wherever he was in the house just to listen to it.

Since it was not really a traditional funeral song, we went for a drive and listened to it to make sure it was appropriate. We cried as we listened and remembered how he swayed to the music. Apart from one or two lines, it was perfect. The song was to be awarded song of the year a few months later at the CMA's. It was "Amazed" by Lonestar.

It occurred to me that it was now, almost a year to the week after I attended church the first time, that I realized why God had led me to his house of worship. We now had a church community to support our family while we grieved and a pastor that knew us and could perform the funeral service.

Amazingly, directly across the lake, at almost the exact same moment that our lives were changed by Travis' accident, 3 members of our church were being baptized that same Sunday morning.

Several members of our church dropped by those first few days, along with our family and several friends. One specific memory, dear to my heart, is of a neighbor who didn't know what to say, so he just walked up to me with a sympathetic smile on his face, holding a box of Kleenex in his outstretched hands. It broke my heart when only a year later, I walked into his home to support their family from a similar tragedy, the loss of their three year old daughter.

I remember my mom and my sisters being there for me, silent, in the background… just watching, helping where they could, making sure all was well, dishes were done, laundry done, kids fed… I remember my dad, always so quiet, watching, making eye contact, sending his love. I remember waking up at 6 AM the day after the accident, looking out the window and seeing my brother walking up my front steps. He was working in the US and had flown home as soon as he could.

Arlen's parents were at their house a block away, greeting, hosting and being consoled by members of their families that lived out of town and would stay for the funeral. Arlen's only brother, Joe, asked if he could pay for Travis' casket and we were deeply touched.

Annie, Trav's little friend from the Shriners had called to see how Travis was and it broke my heart to have to tell her the news. She was so brave on the phone. The Edmonton Sun newspaper called to my parents' house asking about the accident and my aunt, thankfully, gave them a quick comment that satisfied them.

Thankfully, we had many friends stop by that were truly there for us. I don't remember everything, but I do remember when Mike and Nancy walked through the door. They were two of our closest friends and remain our closest friends to this day. Nancy spent endless hours taking walks with me. Both of them let us talk over and over again about our wonderful son; never seeming to tire of the conversations or our grief, although I am sure they were.

I remember another friend, Ginger, who had been very sick, walking through the door. My heart was breaking, but I recall regarding her with great concern because she looked so frail. I also remember someone opening our front door when the doorbell rang, to find the owner of our favorite local pizza place standing there with a stack of about 12 pizzas to feed the mass of people inside. He just said their family sent their love and the pizzas were on the house.

I also remember my friend Rhonda, trying to make me smile and I remember there always being so many people hanging out, just watching and making sure we were ok.

The day our son died, we instantly became part of a special club, the Angel Club. People from our community that had lost children came to our home to share their stories and support us in our grief. We even received cards and letters from people we had never met, welcoming us to the Angel Club. It is strange to be part of a group of people without anything more in common than to have lost a child, but we found comfort and support from them, just knowing we were not alone in our grief.

The night before the funeral, we held a wake at the funeral home. Those that wished to say goodbye were asked to join us. The day was cold and dreary, just as it had been the day of the accident, when I walked into the funeral home to see my middle son's body for the very last time.

His casket was set up at the front of the small room and the lid was open so we could look at his wonderful little face. Arlen put his arm around me as we made our way toward the final bed our son's body would be laid upon. We were both crying as we looked down into the casket.

After looking at him, dressed in his favorite cowboy outfit, wearing his favorite cowboy boots (I couldn't bear to part with his Batman runners and still have them), I reached out and touched his crooked little fingers and held his cold little hands. I looked at his face, now not nearly as swollen as in the trauma room and then I bent over and kissed the soft cool brow of my baby for the very last time.

On the morning of the funeral, I awoke to the same cold and dreariness that I had come to see every day since the accident. It seemed fitting to me; I felt very much that way; cold and dreary. I was grieving and it hurt. I was hurting, yet I was numb. I didn't care how I looked or what I wore that day; yet how I looked and what I wore that day was the most important thing I had to do. I was going to say goodbye to my son in front of our community. I was going to stand up and be seen with my husband and my children so that our family and friends could show us how much they loved my son. To express how much his life had meant to them, how his life had touched theirs, even if in a little way.

When we reached the church, I found June, who I hadn't seen since the accident and asked her to walk in with the family. It was important to me to let people know that we loved and supported June. Barry, her husband, along with another friend named Brian and both our brothers, Joe and Larry, were the pallbearers. June walked down the aisle holding my hand as Arlen walked to my other side, Levi and Devon between us.

A family friend, Peter, was chosen to do a reading and the following is the beautiful Eulogy written by Shawna:

Travis Lane Quartly came into our world on February 8, 1993. He was a proven fighter right from day one. His family was told that he would probably never lift his head; he proved them wrong. The said he wouldn't sit up; he did. The said he wouldn't crawl, but he did. They said that he would never walk without braces, but with numerous surgeries, wheelchairs, casts and pain, again, he proved them wrong. In the dictionary under the word determination, there should be a picture of Travis, as he overcame every obstacle that was ever put before him.

Travis was a very observant little man. After carefully observing whatever it was that he was going to do, he would soon master that task with excitement and joy in his eyes and actions.

After he returned from Sacramento in a wheelchair, Diane brought him to school. She suggested that I take him out of his chair periodically to improve his balance without the braces. Travis had no interest in experimenting with walking in front of his peers. I talked to Diane and Arlen about this and they reassured me that he was working hard on this at home. So sure enough, after one weekend, he returned to school walking better without his braces than he ever had before. He made sure that everyone noticed he was no longer wearing hiking boots, but "hip" new sneakers. This was the start of a very in-style dresser.

The best part about no braces was that he could finally wear cowboy boots and with cowboy boots didn't come sweatpants and a T-shirt. The boots meant sharp jeans, a belt buckle, and a tucked in long sleeve shirt, and of course, a cowboy hat. He slipped and slid, clinked and clanked in those silly boots, but the flawless image of a cowboy was always there.

He also sported his athletic look, which was sneakers, bright white sport socks, sweatpants and a tucked in T-shirt. Oh yes, and of course a backwards baseball cap. I've never met a six year old who was so concerned with his presentation. I soon realized that because he was the most well known little man in the school, he always had to look and act just perfect.

Travis was a fun loving little man with an amazing personality and a great sense of humor. It was impossible to stay upset with Travis for very long because soon after any disciplinary action, you could be sure to expect a swat on the behind and a finger-pointing scolding.

Travis had a real thing for girls young and old. He was always surrounded by girls in the kindergarten room, whether it be playing with their hair or playing in the house center dressed *up in full ladies attire. When flirting with the older women, he was never shy to be picked up, and when he had the chance he would sneak his hand down a blouse or up a skirt.*

Travis had a way of communicating everything without any spoken words. He knew exactly what he wanted and he would be sure to let you know if you were doing anything wrong.

His grandparents took him shopping one day to Costco and started off with putting Travis in the cart while Levi and Devon were hanging on the sides of the cart. Soon, Travis wasn't content with sitting. He got grandma and grandpa to let him hang on the side too; and in no time at all he had one arm up in the air and was yahooing along with his brothers.

Travis had a real ear for music. Whether he was playing on a piano or organ, or just clapping his hands and doing the "Travis Jig". Whenever there was music on in the background, there was always a good chance that you could catch Travis grooving to the tunes. We could all see that music put him in his element.

Travis was a very caring and compassionate little man. He was always more concerned about others. When Travis went anywhere he would make sure that whoever was with him got by safely before continuing. Peers and strangers alike would have to be taken care of first.

*With this quality, it would often take a long time
to walk down the hallways of the school, or through
the lobby of the hockey rink. He had to slap hands
with every child or adult that he met. Travis touched
everyone's heart as he handed out angel dust in the
form of a high-five. He knew when you were sad or
just needed one of his hugs to make you feel better.*

*Somehow, Travis was able to bring out the
best in everyone he encountered and in every
situation he was a part of. All the gifts that we
have been given, Travis had to work for. Watching
Travis experience life and overcoming every
obstacle was nothing less than inspirational. With
all the tough times Travis went through, he always
kept a smile on his face and a sparkle in his eye.
There was no time to waste being sick or sore. He
made every moment count and for every moment
that he was with us, he made us better people.*

*We will never forget you for what you
have taught us and given us. Thank you
Travis—we will miss you and we love you.*

We had chosen only one other song to play at the
funeral, "Amazing Grace"; that along with "Amazed" by
Lonestar, seemed to fit his life.

At one point during the service, I remember seeing a
vision of myself with a cherub over my left shoulder. It
was as if I was standing in front of myself, looking at me.
I can still see that cherub plainly within my mind. In fact,

I can still see that cherub sitting on my shelf at home, because the next day, a flower arrangement showed up at my house with an identical looking little plaster cherub sitting snuggled in the greenery.

Following the ceremony at the church, once we made our way back down the aisle and out to our waiting vehicles, we proceeded in the funeral procession toward the graveyard. We drove near our town office and noticed that the flags were flying at half-mast. We were told later that it was to honor Travis and our families.

The cemetery where our family is laid to rest is located on the east end of town, so we turned onto the main road and continued that way. When we came to the intersection that turned off the main highway onto a secondary road, I was surprised to see an RCMP block the road and salute as we went by. It made me smile a moment to see that the Royal Canadian Mounted Police was Michelle, a close family friend.

The procession stopped and suddenly panic set in. There are two graveyards at the east end of town and it appears that somehow, in our grief and confusion, a mistake had been made. We had chosen the wrong property to lay our son. I was extremely distressed by this; I wanted to change to where my family was, but felt it was too late.

We waited in our vehicles a moment while Travis' casket was unloaded and carried over where it would be set on rollers that would later lower him into the grave. Family and friends who followed in the procession, parked their vehicles and made their way to stand in a semi-circle around the casket, leaving room for us to stand close enough to reach out and touch the smooth, rich wood.

Arlen stood beside me and our boys stood in front of each of us, leaning back against us. The sun broke through the clouds and shone down like gold across the stargazer lilies blanketing the top and draping down the sides of the lacquered wooden box where Travis lay.

There was a house to the right of the graveyard and only a dozen feet from Trav's plot. Behind the fence was a large, black Rottweiler dog and it barked and snarled during the whole internment. I barely noticed it at the time, but Arlen told me later that he could remember nothing of the words spoken by the preacher because he was watching the dog. He was prepared to tackle it, if it jumped the fence and threatened any of us. Levi also recalls nothing of that part of the funeral besides hearing me cry and the dog barking. Thankfully, it never left the confines of its yard and the burial went without further trauma.

I don't remember going home after the funeral. I do remember dropping to my knees and laying my hands in the dirt surrounding the hole as they lowered the casket into the ground.

CHAPTER 7

Awakening to the New Normal

During the days following the funeral, several amazing things began to happen. I saw two distinct "visions". One was of a young man walking towards a light holding the hand of a little boy. I could tell by the way the shadow moved in the vision that the little boy was Travis, and somehow I also knew that the young man walking with him was a boy that had died in an accident as well. The young man worked for the trucking company my husband managed.

The second vision was of a lady sitting on a chair, holding a little boy on her lap. Again, I knew the boy was Travis and I also knew that the lady was a friend of mine who had passed only a few months earlier. She had been the victim of a random attack while jogging one morning and she didn't survive. Her husband told me he sat outside our house several hours before he was able to come inside to express his condolences; his pain was still so acute, his grief still so new.

It was this friend, who is also a doctor that brought us a little bit of peace in the face of this terrible accident.

He told us during his visit that he had reviewed Travis' accident and came to the conclusion that "even if the accident had happened just outside the double doors of the hospital, they still would not have been able to save Travis." As horrible as this sounds, it actually gave Arlen and me some comfort in knowing that the outcome wouldn't have changed regardless of anything anyone did immediately following the accident.

I could not get these two visions out of my mind. They kept playing over and over again until one day I sketched them into a journal. Somehow, by putting them on paper, I was able to release them from my mind. I have the sketches to remind me of what I saw, but I can bring those images to mind anytime at all.

Another thing that happened, was that a vision of one of those old café flip menus played around and around in my head. It was like a list, flipping over and around. Travis, Travis, Travis... For many days and nights I awoke and went to sleep with that chart flipping and flipping in my brain.

A few days after the funeral, I decided I wanted to go to visit Travis' grave on my own. I pulled up and drove through the cemetery gate, which was always left open, and stopped a few feet from Trav's spot. The sun was out and I felt the heat on my face as I stepped out of my vehicle.

All of a sudden, the dog that had been so distracting at the funeral, ran from behind its house and lunged at the fence. He was big and he was aggressive. I was terrified and jumped quickly back into my van. Every time I tried to visit for the next few weeks, I would sit in my vehicle, too scared to get out because that dog was always there. He would snarl and bark at the fence whenever I tried to leave my vehicle. I have always been terrified of dogs, so I would just sit in the driver's seat and cry; time after time.

I went to our town office after about 2 weeks to see if there was anything they could do, but they would not help. Imagine not being able to sit at your son's grave and pray in silence. Imagine fearing for your safety every time you left your vehicle.

It was a couple of months later when I realized it was the dog that was keeping me from visiting the grave. I know now that this was a blessing in disguise. I'm certain that I would have basically lived there every day if it had not been for fear of this dog. Pining away and grieving; I can even imagine myself asleep, lying beside his mound of dirt. At almost the exact same time that I realized this, made peace with this, the people that rented the home moved. The dog was no longer there.

We did find out some time later that a lady who had gone to visit her husband's grave, a short distance from Trav's, was in fact attacked by this dog and had to have several stitches to close her wounds.

This was also the time when I began sketching the images of my visions as well as the image of Trav's name on the flip menu that was going over and over in my brain. As soon as I put them down on paper, I was able to release them.

My journey of healing began and as I went through the motions of everyday life for my husband and two little boys, my life started to change; my ideals and beliefs about life after death started to change.

One day, while sitting in my kitchen, just a few days after the funeral, I looked over at the wall above our stairwell and saw an angel. It was a ceramic "Welcome to Our Home" angel and I was astounded to realize that June had given me that angel for Christmas that same year. It then hit me, somewhat like a punch in the gut, that Travis had given me a gold Angel pin that very same Christmas as well. Those were the first 2 angels I had ever received as gifts. After that I became somewhat obsessed with them. People started giving me angels as gifts and on cards and to this day, they still do.

I didn't leave the house the days following the funeral and if I had to buy groceries, I would make my way to our twenty-four hour grocery store at midnight. I found it easier on me, as well as the people of my community, to do my shopping then.

People never knew what to say to me and it actually became quite amusing when I saw someone turn the corner down the aisle and see me; they would get a horrified look on their face and you could tell they wanted to run. I think they just found it so uncomfortable to approach someone who was grieving; they didn't know what to say or how to react. I usually ended up starting a conversation or I just said, "hi" in order to ease their discomfort, but what I really wanted to do was yell, "Boo!"

About a week after the funeral, I gathered money and checks that were given to us to take to the bank as we had setup an account so that donations could be made in Travis' name to the Shriners. It was the first time besides trips to the cemetery or the midnight grocery runs, that I had gone anywhere since the funeral.

After making the deposits, as I was walking out of the bank through the first set of double doors, I happened to look at a poster that was on the entryway wall. It was a poster that included pictures of about 20 missing kids and showed what they might look like today. I lost it.

I started crying, actually sobbing, because my heart hurt so badly for those parents. I realized in that moment, that even though I had just been through something so horrible, these people were going through something possibly worse. I knew what happened to my little boy, I knew where his body lay; and I knew that I could grieve for him. I can't begin to imagine the pain these parents were going through and continue to go through.

At that moment, I realized that there is always something worse; someone, somewhere is always going through something worse. There was a lady outside the bank that day that comforted me, although I can't remember who she was. I do hope I thanked her for her kindness.

Life without Travis began, I was happy to let my bosses take care of any real estate deals I had to finish and I concentrated on just functioning; keeping things together for my family.

One night I awoke to the sound of gentle sobs coming from Levi and Devon's room. We had a four level split layout in our home and because there were only two large bedrooms on the upper floor, all three of our boys shared a room. Travis' bed now lay empty and Levi and Devon shared bunks. Devon slept on the top, which was a single bed, while Levi was on the bottom in a double bunk. Because Levi's was such a big bed, Travis would often leave his bed to crawl in and sleep with him during the night.

As I entered their room, I found Levi lying in bed crying, his pillow wet with tears. I hugged him a moment before I asked what was wrong and it broke my heart to hear his response.

One of our dear friends had brought a stuffed pony for Devon and a stuffed Lion to Levi after the funeral. The lion that was given to Levi had a rough and unruly main of hair and apparently, Levi had woken to the lion's main tickling his nose. He was sobbing because for just one split second, he thought it was Travis' hair that was tickling him. He was so heartbroken and it made me so sad. I hugged him to comfort him as best I could, and then laid down beside him to sleep.

It was about two weeks after the funeral that our dear friend Tracy, the one whose family had been camping with us the weekend of the accident, called to tell us that she had written a letter to the local radio station where she lived. The station was having a contest and the winner would win tickets to see Lonestar. They happened to be touring in a city that was a two-hour drive from where we lived. Tracy told us that, although we hadn't won the contest, the radio station wanted to send us to the concert and even gave us the opportunity to meet the band before the show.

The very next day, Arlen and I drove the 2 hours to Grande Prairie where the lady from the radio station met us and then led us backstage to meet the band. When we got there, she read the letter that Tracy had sent to them. It was a wonderful letter that told about Travis, his life, how precious he was and the significance of the song "Amazed".

There were many tears and we stood with the band so a picture could be taken. I remember apologizing to the band for bringing such a sad mood to them just before they got on stage; poor guys. One of the band members, Dean Samms, seemed especially upset and explained that his wife had just had their first daughter, so he was feeling extremely saddened by our story.

We were ushered out to the concert and stood in the second row, center. I was in a bit of a daze, but the concert was awesome and we were so thankful to be there. When they played "Amazed", Richie, the lead singer, moved to the far right end of the stage and none of the band made eye contact with us. It was a good thing, because we had tears in our eyes and could barely kept it together!

By the end of their concert, we were exhausted and a little overwhelmed by the whole evening. The band left the stage and of course, cheering began for an encore. We had just turned to leave when they returned to the stage. We were exhausted, but decided we could handle it as they played a couple more songs and then, to everyone's utter delight, they started to play "Amazed" again.

This time, near the end of the song, the lyrics were "every little thing that you do, baby, I'm amazed by you"; the boys in the band all came to stand directly in front of us at the center of the stage and sang "every little thing that you do, Travis, we're all amazed by you". My heart soared, my mind went blank and I will forever be grateful to those wonderful, wonderful men for that moment! Of course, we cried and people around us had tears in their eyes as well.

Within two weeks, Arlen was back at work, family and friends resumed life and we made the best of our new normal. Part of that new normal was spending time with Barry and June. We invited them over to our house for supper one evening and I remember June and me sitting on our front step watching the kids play in the yard. I recall her saying, "I know there will come a time when you will be very angry with me, you will hate me and I accept that, I expect that."

At the time, I told her that the only thing that would make me angry was if she let her family or herself, fall apart. I said that I did not want my son's name associated with the breakdown of her family or with the ruin of her life. I told her to live a good, healthy life in his honor. I expected her to keep it together for him.

To this day, I can honestly say that June's prediction or expectation never came true. I have never hated her for the accident; of course, I realize the part she played in the events that day, just as I realize the circumstances of everyone's actions that day, but there is no hatred, no anger.

I know Arlen felt and still feels some guilt for not watching closer, just as I am sure all the adults there that day do. We spoke of Arlen's guilt just once. We knew that because of his disability and problems balancing, Travis would often stand at the bumper of vehicles for stability; the height was just right for him. We had noticed this and moved him from the back of vehicles a thousand times, but the accident still happened. I told him that I believed it was Travis' time to go and to carry guilt over it would only hurt all of us. We needed to remember Travis with only the energy of love.

Levi told me years later, actually, while we discussed this book and as I wrote it, that he felt guilty because he and all the other kids left Travis with Arlen and Mel that day at Barry and June's lot to go play; he felt he was the big brother and should have taken care of him, taken him with them. It makes me so sad to think that he carried that kind of guilt with him all these years. He was just a little boy and it certainly wasn't his responsibility.

My perspective of life changed, I've changed. I was forced to handle some extremely hard issues. I was forced to look at my simple little life, my easy going little family and the people in my life; the influences in my life. When you lose a child, your focus becomes very selfish and even though I was going through the motions of being a wife and a mother. I was also feeling things at a level a hundred times more than before. I was processing things differently and I was reacting to things differently.

The problem for me was that people simply carried-on with their lives and over time, they forgot I was still hurting and grieving. They would often look at me like I was just a selfish, angry person, and maybe I was. I now know that throughout all this misery of interacting with certain people, something very spiritual was happening in my life.

We attended church the Sunday following the accident and this managed to stop our minister right in his tracks when he noticed us. I think he was surprised to see us there so soon, but it seemed to me to be the natural thing to do. My church family was there for us and I had deep faith in the knowledge that God had guided us to this place. He guided us here almost exactly a year before so that we would have this place to visit and heal; so that we would have these people to share our journey with. It was a beautiful service. During the next few Sundays, I felt more connected than ever to God and our church.

I stood at my bathroom mirror one day and I remember looking into the mirror at this broken soul, my broken soul. I looked at my eyes and they seemed lost, distant somehow. I looked at my skin, hollow and pale. There was no light there, but I was speaking to God. I was questioning him as to why this was happening? Why did it happen? What lesson was I supposed to learn? What was I being punished for? And then it happened…

I realized that God *was* answering me. Not in a big booming voice, not in a vision or even a sign, but in my thoughts, in my feelings, and the way I was changing. I knew, deep in my soul that I wasn't being punished. My God is a loving God and wouldn't punish me by taking my son away. That was not the God I believed in. That was not the God I loved.

What lessons was I to learn? What life experience was I to figure out? Well, here it is: Pay attention to the little things. Love your people, your family every day. Hold on to the things and people you love and appreciate them. Make time to enjoy the silly, crazy, happy times. Take time to laugh, sing, and play with your people. Notice all the wonderful things. The way they sound even when they are crying. Remember everything. Remember their facial expressions, even when they are angry. Trust me, those are the greatest memories. Those are the greatest things to remember.

That is the lesson I learned most by losing my son. As an example, before his accident, I only had perfect pictures out around my house, of perfect poses, beautiful smiles and tidy spaces. However, after the accident, I cherished the pictures where Travis' face was screwed up in laughter because I could hear the sound he made when he did that. The picture when he was pinching his cousin's butt is one of my favorites now. That time he looked pensively out the window. Why hadn't I noticed that picture before?

The one where he was trying to put on his brothers skates and stand up was so funny and endearing now, but was shoved into a box back then because he wasn't wearing pants, just a T-shirt and a diaper. I didn't want anyone to see that I let my kids walk around without pants on in the house. I also had beautiful pictures of my kids beautiful smiles or laughter, but never put those pictures out; because there was an untidy space behind them and I wouldn't want anyone else to judge my housekeeping skills.

I look at those things now and realize that they were my own judgments of myself. I didn't care when I went to a friend's house that they had laundry piled on the couch to be folded. Why did I think they would care if my house wasn't perfect either?

These are the realizations I had after losing my son. It was all about the simple things, things that stressed me out. Things that I felt defined me. I was able to realize in the hours, days, months and years after his death that those things truly were not worth stressing over. I knew in my heart all along that they really didn't matter. I just made them matter by putting that pressure on myself. The pressure came from holding myself to an unrealistic and impossible standard. Don't get me wrong, I still like to have a clean and tidy home, but not for fear of judgment from anyone else.

I go back to that in my mind often. I imagine myself standing in front of the mirror in that house where we no longer live and I remember... I absorb the feeling! It helps me to focus my mind on love, on perfect light!

A few Sundays later, I was overcome with that same feeling during a church service. I recall looking around, feeling sorry for everyone there, because I felt like I "got it", like I was somehow more connected; it was a feeling of pure bliss!

It was during these days that I began to reflect on some unexplainable incidents that happened in the years before. I always knew I had a strong sense of intuition, I always knew I was connecting to Spirit in some way, I just thought everyone could.

The first incident happened regarding Arlen's cousin, Curtis. I had only met him a couple of times, but thought he was a special soul. Sadly, he was in the hospital, fighting a terminal illness and we really only got reports of his progress every couple of weeks.

One night, I awoke just after 1:00 AM, to a vision of a man standing in the doorway to our bedroom. The room was lit behind him and our room was dark, so I was only able to see a silhouette of the man. He stood facing me, standing to one side within the doorway, in a long overcoat and he wore a fedora. I heard the words "he's gone" and I knew it was Curtis who had passed. I woke Arlen the next morning and told him what I saw and an hour later, we got the phone call telling us Curtis had passed during the night, at the exact time I had my vision.

Another time, I awoke at 3:00 in the morning to a vision of my grandmother, my dad's mom, standing at the end of my bed. It was strange, because I was awake. It was so "real" that my first thought was, "how did she get into our house?" because I knew the door was locked.

My second thought, because of my experience with Arlen's cousins passing, was that perhaps she had passed away. I called her early the next morning and was happy to hear her voice. I told her of my vision and she nonchalantly replied, "That would have been about 3:00, my legs were a bit restless, so I probably needed a walk." I loved that! I loved that my 85-year-old grandmother was so open to the idea of spirit travel.

Another spiritual awakening for me was my paintings. About a year before Trav's transition, during the times we were struggling with raising three children and establishing our way in the world, I grabbed a board and painted the words "God Gives Us Only That Which We Can Handle". It kind of became our family motto.

I hung the sign in our Kitchen and whenever someone was complaining about something or was feeling sorry for themselves, we would just point at the sign. That sign became so much more to us after Travis was gone. It hangs in our kitchen to this day and is a constant reminder of God's belief in our strength.

Although I felt tired most of the time, sleeping was something that wouldn't always come. I recall one particular night, when I had finally fallen asleep, only to awaken at four in the morning to a pillow, soaked with tears. Travis would often get up during the night, if his feet were especially sore after a long and active day, and would come to our room. He would silently stand beside my bed, not making the slightest sound, looking at me sleep until I inevitably felt his presence and woke up. I somehow felt him and would know he was there, but before I ever opened my eyes. When I did open them, every time, he would startle me and I would gasp. This was always fun for him and he would giggle.

I would sit up so that he could grab hold and crawl in behind my back and settle down between Arlen and me. He would lay his head on Arlen's shoulder and put his broken little feet towards me so that I could rub and massage the hurt away.

This time, when I opened my eyes after waking and feeling his presence, my little man was nowhere to be found. It took a moment for me to get my bearings and realize that he would never, ever, be standing at the side of my bed again.

Sometimes because I couldn't sleep, I would spend hours painting during the night. It was something I could do to help me focus on something other than my grief. I, of course, was obsessed with angels and so I painted angels.

The first one I painted was of an angel walking in the snow, looking around a tree at a butterfly that was flying away. I know now that the picture is a depiction of the way I was feeling at the time; of me observing my dear Travis' flying away, his transition. It is amazing how our spirit works and how that act of painting was so much more than just putting paint to paper.

One of the other angel paintings I did was given to friends who had lost 2 children at birth. It was the very couple I did a reading for at the beginning of this story, because Jodi was drawn to it. Another was given to my father, who felt a connection to it.

Art became part of my healing process and allowed me to connect with my soul at a deeper level. It also allows me to remember that time of healing whenever I am drawn to look at that picture of the winter angel. It hangs in my home and although it is visible every day, there are times when I still find myself standing in front of it, looking at it. It brings great comfort to me. It's usually those days when I know that Travis is sending his love. Those paintings were therapeutic to me and I am blessed to have them as a reminder of that time of healing.

Another symbol of love and a lesson in memories came from my cousin, Gaylene. At that time, she lived with her family in Texas. I never wanted to leave my house without something that belonged to Travis; I always felt a need to carry something of my little mans. Whether it be a picture or his glasses, I always wanted something of his with me everywhere I went. I needed to be holding something of his, a part of him, or I felt panic set in.

The day I received a card and package in the mail from Gaylene, my panic ended. Included in the package was a silver heart on a long sturdy chain. On the front of the heart, stamped into the metal it reads "The Heart Remembers" and on the back, my wonderful cousin had Trav's name and date of birth as well as the date of his death engraved on it. There was also a small star hanging on the chain as well.

From that day on, I was able to leave the pictures and possessions of my little man at home. The necklace somehow gave me a sense that I carried a part of him with me whenever I wore it. I wear that necklace almost every day still. The engraving on the back has almost worn off, but it remains engraved in my soul. Such a blessing!

Gaylene sent a pair of little silver cowboy boots a year later that reminded her of a picture of Travis we have where he is standing watching the parade at our local rodeo, the month before he died. He was so proud to be able to wear those cowboy boots and that picture of him was put on the front of his funeral card. I attached the boots to my keychain and had them there for years until someone stole them at a gathering. I am sad and I hope the energy of love in those boots help the person who took them in some way.

A month after the funeral, I was once again compelled to write. I sat down at my kitchen table and the following words came to me:

Today has been a really hard day,
It's been one month since you passed away.
My heart grows full as I think of your smile
And I cry a bit every once in a while.
You taught us so much without saying a word,
You couldn't speak, yet everyone heard.
Messages taught rang out loud and clear,
One look in your eyes and we never needed to hear.
You showed us how to live just for that day,
Without worry or self-pity, you led the way.
Never questioning the journey that fate handed you;
Living each moment as exciting and new.
The path often involved a hard hill to climb,
But you carried on, never seeming to mind.
Although so much wisdom appeared locked inside,
Your Spirit showed through, refusing to hide.
We worked on the package that your soul came wrapped in,
Seeing the spirit and beauty within.

We loved every part that made you complete,
Each crooked little finger to both mended feet.
With every new sunrise for seasons to come,
We'll be planning our days while missing someone.
Such a great soul was God's gift to us;
For six blessed years, He put you into our trust.
So we must rejoice and give thanks each day,
For every moment we had, before you went away.
Every tear that falls from our eyes as if rain,
Will be replaced by a rainbow when we see you again.
A lifetime shall pass until once more we meet,
So, we'll keep you in our hearts to
keep our family complete.

CHAPTER 8

Drawing on Angels

Time moved slowly for us those first few months. The boys went back to school and I returned to work long enough to finish up my open real estate accounts. I decided to quit my job and be at home for my family. Arlen was back to working full time and the days moved forward.

One evening after putting the boys to bed for the night, Arlen told me about an incredible thing that had happened that day. He met that afternoon with his parents at a local restaurant for some coffee and a visit when an acquaintance they knew, came over to sit with them. The man seemed very agitated and all at once started to cry. He told them that he had a dream a couple of nights earlier and in the dream he saw a boy who he believes was Travis. He said he didn't recognize the boy at first who was standing on a boulder wearing sweatpants, running shoes and no shirt. The little boy was posing on top of a boulder flexing his muscles like a body builder would and said, "Tell my mommy and daddy that I'm really strong now, my body is really strong."

The man was visibly upset and said that he didn't know who the boy's parents were until he saw Travis' funeral announcement in the newspaper the day before. He then knew he had to come over and tell the story as soon as he saw Arlen and his parents enter the restaurant. They could tell it was an extremely hard thing for him to do.

That October we received another message from our little man. One day when we were at the arena for one of Arlen's hockey games, a lady acquaintance from town, told me about how her sister also had a dream where she saw Travis sitting up in a hospital bed looking really good. There were children all around the bed, laughing and talking and excited that he was there. Travis was giggling and happy; holding a ragged, little brown teddy bear.

I was shocked when I heard that last bit of the dream. The teddy bear they described matched the one that June had put into his casket the night before his funeral. Only a couple of us even knew that June had put that teddy bear in the casket. It was messages like these that were beginning to have a significant impact on my consciousness as well as opening me more and more to the idea of communicating with spirit. While they were seemingly random and from people we hardly knew, I felt like spirit was definitely trying to communicate with me.

In November of 1999, just a short 3 months after our lives changed, we decided a family trip to Disneyland might be a good idea. There had been so much sadness in all our lives. Our little boys, who were just 8 and 5 dearly needed a bit of happiness and to just be kids again.

Arlen's parents came with us and for 7 days we headed on a family adventure.

We chose a Canadian airline and had a horrible experience. Our flight had been overbooked and we were given a different flight, which was not direct. This cost us an extra day of travel to LA as well as on our return home. This was very upsetting because we had booked our flight so that we would arrive in LA early the first morning and depart late the last evening. This way we could spend almost 6 full days in LA. Unfortunately, with the change, we ended up spending the first day flying from Edmonton to Calgary and arriving on the second day in LA late in the afternoon. Our return flight was the same way. Together these delays cut short our trip by two full days. It was so disappointing that we were only spending 4 days there.

Needless to say, it was exasperating, so I wrote a letter to the airline explaining our circumstances. In truth this was really just a way for me to release some of my pent-up frustration. However, I was incredibly surprised when they sent us free tickets (for each of us) to fly anywhere within the next year that their airline flew! We were very pleased and booked a return trip to LA for the end of the following January to the beginning of February. This time, we booked a full 10 days and took the boys to Sea World in San Diego and Legoland in Carlsbad. It was a wonderful trip and it was there that I had a sort of epiphany.

While I stood in line with my boys, waiting to see Mickey Mouse, I realized that I was terribly sad that Travis wasn't with us. It was at that moment that I also realized that I wasn't sad that Travis wasn't there to meet Mickey Mouse that day, I was sad because I wasn't able to *see* him meet Mickey Mouse that day!

The thought came to me that it was my own selfishness that was causing my sadness. Travis was actually there with us in spirit; he could meet Mickey Mouse whenever he wanted now, I truly believe that. It led me to think deeper about this and to recognize that, as a parent, my little boy, who had suffered through a large part of his short life on earth, would never have to feel pain or discomfort again. It was just my own selfishness that wanted him to remain on earth. After all, where else would any parent want their child to be other than in the most safe, secure, loving arms of God in heaven? My life changed just a little bit on that day.

I knew from then on that it is the memories we share and keep that are what is most important, not the actual, physical body and material things that belonged to our loved ones.

I was finally able to start giving away toys and possessions that belonged to Travis, so that they could be used and enjoyed by others. I recognize that this is one of the more difficult things for a parent who has lost a child to do and this spiritual shift of understanding was significant for me. I realized that if I took a picture of whatever it was, the picture was enough to remind me of what I needed to keep close in my heart. The picture was enough to give me the same feeling of love that the actual item had given me. The memory was the important part, not the physical item. What a freeing thought.

That first Christmas came and went with such mixed emotions. One of the hardest things about losing a child is to "remove" them from your life. The big things are done for you; the government "removes" your dependent child, healthcare "removes" your dependent child, but when it comes to signing your first Christmas card… this I found to be one of the hardest things to do.

My children were 8, 6 and 5 when the accident happened to take our beautiful boy home to heaven. At that time, I was either still signing the boys' names to any cards I sent out to family and friends, or tracing their handprint with their name in the middle.

I will never forget when I went to sign that first card; I wrote "Love Arlen, Diane, Levi…" my hand froze. How could I possibly just "remove" my son? How could I delete, eliminate, not write his name, like he didn't exist? My solution to my mini meltdown was to draw a little angel where I would have put Trav's name.

From that day on, that little angel became a symbol of Travis to me and my family. My sister has added Trav's little blue angel to a tattoo on her leg, my niece has his angel tattooed on her wrist, and I also have Trav's little blue angel tattooed on my left shoulder.

We had decided, in honor of Travis and the Shriners and all they had done for us, to host a party on Dec. 22nd. We felt this date worked best, because Travis had died on the 22nd of August. The party was to be a gathering and celebration of his life. We supplied all the food and drinks and asked that anyone who attended bring a new children's book to be donated to a local hospital in Travis' name.

The following is a copy of the letter we sent with the box of books to the hospital:

> *Our family was blessed with the birth of our second of three sons on Feb. 8th 1993. Travis was a wonderful and happy boy who had many friends and family; unfortunately, Travis also had Trisomy 9p. While Travis was having surgery to repair his feet at the Shriners hospital in Sacramento, California, we really got to know the loving and caring people involved with the Shriners. Travis was thrilled whenever the "fuzzy hats" came around to his room, usually bearing small gifts. One day, he received a wooden truck, another, a small book and was even lucky enough to receive a homemade quilt and hand knitted socks to cover the casts on his feet. It was a wonderful environment for healing.*

> *On August 22, 1999, Travis was in a traffic accident and left us. We still have heavy hearts, but amazing memories of a boy who could not talk, but spoke*

volumes, could not write, but made beautiful
pictures; was kind, gentle and touched so many
in our community with his soulful presence.

In memory of Travis, and with appreciation for all
that the Shriners did for our family, we host a party
on Dec. 22nd each year. We call it Trav's Book
Party, but many refer to it as our "Angel Party".
We supply food and beverages and all who come
are asked to bring a children's book to donate to
a local hospital. Each year the number of books
grows and we are thrilled with the response.

Rather than have the books left on tables and
counters within the hospitals, we love to see them
given to children to take home with them.

From our hearts to yours...

We have continued this tradition every year since and
have donated thousands of books in Travis' name.

On Christmas day, some members of our immediate
family went with us to Travis' grave to say Merry Christmas
and let him know we were thinking of him. When we
arrived at the site, I noticed a small Christmas tree had
been decorated with homemade ornaments and left in
front of his headstone. It was beautiful and I knew it had
been decorated with love.

When I looked at the back of one of the little paper ornaments, I saw written on the back "Love, the Michaelsons." June and her family had left the little tree and it made me extremely happy.

I returned to the grave a week after Christmas and brought the little tree home. Most of the ornaments had been wrecked due to the winter weather, but the one with that sentiment on the back remained unscathed. I put that little tree out, including the paper ornament, every year. It sits beside Travis' picture and reminds me of the kindness of their family and the little bit of joy it brought to me that Christmas day so many years ago.

It was in July that following year of the accident that Arlen's parents had taken our boys with them to a family picnic, which happened every year in central Alberta. Arlen was working and unable to go but we thought it would be nice for the boys to get away camping for the weekend with their grandparents. They had a great time and were to arrive home on the Sunday night, although we weren't sure as to when to expect them.

After having supper and doing the dishes, Arlen and I sat down to watch TV and wait for them. All of a sudden, I got really anxious. I started pacing and looking out the window, feeling really uneasy. Arlen asked what I was doing and I told him how I was feeling. Although he reasoned that his parents often took their time travelling and were always late for most things, he couldn't hide the worry that was evident in his eyes. He knew that I had always been intuitive and that intuition had been especially acute since the accident. We tried to call their cell phone and received no answer.

Another hour passed before the phone rang, startling us both. It was Arlen's dad and he was calling from the hospital. He quickly told Arlen that he and the boys were fine, but that they had been in an accident and Arlen's mom was being checked out for injuries.

We ran the half block to the hospital; fear gripping so tight I felt I could choke on it. When I saw my boys standing in the emergency room, I ran to them and hugged them tight. After scanning their little bodies for injuries, I hugged them again and turned to my father-in-law. He said that they were just a few miles out of town when the accident occurred.

Apparently, an oncoming car had stopped at an intersection, waiting to turn into a gas station across the highway in front of them. It was dusk and the person driving the vehicle behind them did not see this car stopped and ran into the back of it. This pushed their small vehicle across the road, right in front of Arlen's parents and the boys. There was nowhere for Rick, Arlen's dad, to go with the big dual wheeled pickup he was driving while also pulling a fifth wheel camper. The momentum forced them right over the small car that was pushed in front of them. The camper they were pulling, pushed up and over the pickup, which went over the car and everything ended up on it's side in the ditch.

We waited at the hospital until we were told that Arlen's mom, Trudy was fine except for some bruising before we all went back to our place to hear the rest of the story.

Rick recounts that once the truck came to a stop, lying on its side, Levi was the first to get out of his seatbelt and stand up on the door, which was now lying on the ground. Being the wise and old soul that he is, he looked around for a few moments before saying "Actually Papa, I think we can get out through here" pointing to the side window that had been broken and was now directly above them. Rick managed to untangle himself from the wheel and by that time, Levi had helped Devon get free. Trudy was in pain and crumpled into a bit of a ball. Unfortunately, she hadn't been wearing her seatbelt.

Rick managed to lift Levi and Devon up far enough that they were able to climb out of the window above them and then he turned his attention to Trudy. By this time, the ambulance had arrived at the scene and all available hands were busy extracting Trudy from the wreckage.

Tragically, the elderly couple who were in the small car that was pushed in front of them, died immediately at the scene. I was horrified to find out later by one of the lady workers of the gas station that she found Levi standing beside the couple's car, staring at them, before she took both Devon and Levi away from the scene and watched after them until they were taken to the hospital.

That night, once everyone had left and we had tucked our boys safely into their beds, I remember feeling how very lucky I was. I also remember thinking how insane it was to be feeling I was lucky at all, considering what my family had been through within the last few months. My soul was feeling things that my "thinking brain" had to adjust to. Although my mind was racing with all of the possible tragic outcomes that could have been, my soul was letting me know that all was well.

CHAPTER 9

Paying Attention

The days leading up to the first anniversary of Travis' accident, only 10 short days after our wedding anniversary, found everyone in our house in a melancholy mood. We moped around and anticipated the sadness to be somehow worse that day than any other day. It's strange how a date on the calendar can cause a change in energy. I personally began to ask God for a sign, some proof that Heaven existed. I knew it did, but at that time, I just wanted something more. I wanted proof and something (anything) to let me know that Travis was still around us. I needed to know that he was all right, that he knew that we were thinking of him and hoping that he was thinking of us.

On the evening of August 21st (just one day before Travis' anniversary), while family was visiting, I suddenly got the urge to get up from the table where we were having coffee and walked over to our south-facing window. I stood there and notice something startling.

Now, because the sun shone and reflected off our pale yellow siding on that part of the house, it always proved impossible to grow flowers of any sort in the beds below that big window. There were, however, hedges and even a tree at the corner. In fact, I have a picture of our three sons standing in front of that tree, all with their arms around one another; Travis' nose is swollen in the picture because it was taken shortly after the quad accident. However, there are no flowers in sight.

That night, peeking out from beneath that tree, was one long stem, with two flower buds! I was amazed. Yet, I instinctually knew that those 2 buds would open the next day, one year to the day of Travis's death. I also intuitively knew that they would be stargazer lilies. I couldn't help but ask myself if this was the sign I had been praying for?

The next morning, lying in bed contemplating the realization that a full year of grief had passed, I suddenly remembered the buds and ran downstairs to look. There they were; two amazing and beautiful stargazer lilies, deep fuchsia in color, reaching out from beneath that bush. Even if someone had wanted too, there is no way they could have planted a seed for a stargazer lily and planned to have it opened *that* day. I knew it was a miracle and an incredible sign of love from God and my son!

Being an artist, I did paint a picture with those two stargazer lilies and have that picture hanging in my studio still. It always seemed unfinished until only a few months ago when I painted one lone, blue butterfly in the top corner. The picture is now complete.

It was during the spring of that first year when I knew it was time to try and bring some happiness back into the lives of my family. So, I had decided that I would buy an English bulldog puppy for Arlen for our anniversary;

Arlen had always wanted a bulldog. I contacted a breeder and found out that they were expecting a litter of puppies that would be ready to go by the middle of August. Our anniversary is August 12th, so that was perfect.

The boys could barely contain their excitement about this and I was so proud of them for keeping the surprise a secret from their dad. The puppies were born on my birthday, June 23rd and I put a down payment on one. I managed to take the boys to meet and pick out the puppy when he was only a few weeks old. They picked a little male and decided his name should be Rocky. He was the runt of the litter and he was perfect.

When the day came that we were to pick him up to bring him home, we told my husband about the gift and he was stunned; the boys were crazy excited. We made the trip to the kennel to bring him home. As we filled out the paperwork and made the final payment, I found it ironic that Rocky was the 22nd puppy born to the sire and so his tattoo was K22.

The number 22 had been showing up in our lives so often, Devon was born on Jan. 22nd, Travis died on Aug. 22, every hotel room we had, including on our Disneyland adventures had been either 322 or 122; countless other 22 signs had shown up.

Rocky was gentle and he was adorable. I was shocked at how quickly the energy in our home rose to a new and happier level. He seemed to make every day just a little brighter, a little lighter. He was such a great addition to our family and was so well behaved. He never left the boundary of our yard *ever*, even when other dogs walked by; he simply ignored them.

That summer following his arrival, Rocky was outside in the back yard playing with our boys and a few kids from the neighborhood. I was in front of the house weeding beneath some shrubs and Arlen was cleaning and organizing the garage. We could hear the kids laughing in the back, when all of a sudden I heard tires squealing. To my shock, I heard June yelling "Diane!" Hearing her call my name like this immediately made my blood run cold as I instantly flashed back to the hospital and the moment of the doctor's pronouncement of Travis. I turned around and started running as I yelled, "Oh my God, not again!"

While working in the front yard, I hadn't noticed that June was walking her new little puppy on a leash across the other side of the road. Rocky uncharacteristically bolted across the road to meet with them. Just then, a small car was driving along and screeched to a stop, but unfortunately, still hitting Rocky.

Fortunately, being that he's an English bulldog, he is very muscular and has a bit of padding to protect him. He rolled into a ball, just barely managing to escape the front tires, and spun in front of it. When he stopped rolling, he jumped up, bolted for the house, ran up the stairs straight onto the couch. He just sat there as we ran to him. He was panting and there was blood dripping from some wounds where the skin had been scraped off.

Arlen immediately took him to the vet while I calmed all the kids down. June was understandably upset. When the kids were settled and we waited for Arlen to call or return home, I remember thinking that the person in the car probably had quite a scare, however, they continued on their way as soon as Rocky bolted.

It was a couple of hours later that Arlen returned home with our wonderful Rocky. He was sore and he was scared, but he would be fine.

I often wonder, to this day, what it was that made Rocky run across the road to greet June. He didn't really know her because our families hadn't spent time together since he joined our family and he had never paid attention to anyone walking past our yard before. Knowing what I now know about energetic associations, I can only speculate that he felt drawn to her because our families are forever connected.

Over the next few years, life continued without Travis here in the physical world, however, we spoke of him often and included him in as many ways as we could. I would buy a book on his birthday to add to the Angel Party collection donated at Christmas and each birthday we celebrated with adding him to the "Candle Race".

This is a family tradition where we take the candles off whoever's birthday cake we are celebrating and stand them up on a wooden board. Once they are secured, we number each one. Then each person picks a candle that they believe will last the longest before burning out. We then light them and watch the candles burn down as we eat our cake. The winner always gets bragging rights.

We always assign Travis a number and honestly, he has won more races than anyone else to date. Quite often, as we played the candle race game, we would have CMT, the country music station, playing in the background and more than once, "Amazed" by Lonestar would suddenly be playing. It would bring us to tears every time! Thank you Travis.

As we continued to keep Travis' memory alive in our home, we were often surprised when others thought to include him in theirs.

We were excited one day when our friends Mel and Tracy called to say that they were expecting their fourth child. Tracy told me that a few days before she found out she was pregnant, she had a dream and in the dream was told she would have a baby boy and that they would call him Harrison Travis Dean and that's exactly what they did!

We were thrilled to have a beautiful baby boy named after Travis, but it didn't end there. Shawna, Travis' aid at school, sent me a note after she had her third daughter. She said that they had been hoping for a boy through all three pregnancies because they had wanted to name their son after Travis. When they had the third girl they decided to name her Sage Alaina after him. Travis' middle name is Laine.

Shortly after that, when my brother and his wife had their first child, a boy, they called him Brock Travis George. So, to this day, there are three beautiful children named after our wonderful son who lived a full six years; what a legacy; we are delighted.

In the years that followed, my growing awareness of angels, spirit messages and signs increased my yearning to connect more with Source. I spent years watching psychic mediums like, John Edward, who had given me new spiritual concepts to explore. My personal study of the angelic realm by reading books from authors and teachers like Doreen Virtue, gave me hope and a better understanding of where my son now lived, in the non-physical.

In 2008, I attended a workshop facilitated by Dawn. She was the beautiful lady who brought Travis to me from the other side for the first time during that first reading I had several months before.

Dawn had blown my mind when she had brought my little man through to me those months before, saying, "He's here." During that reading, I heard her give messages to me directly from Travis. He spoke, through her, of his life, what we as a family meant to him, his pride for how we were continuing to honor him every day and the love that he had for us.

I sat, hanging onto every word and when the reading was over, gave her a hug filled with awe and gratitude.

I had driven the hour home in a state of shock to then recount all that I had experienced to Arlen. It gave us such an incredible feeling of peace, and for me, it heightened my curiosity of the world of spirits and metaphysics. I craved more knowledge on the subjects of angels and the afterlife and I prayed to have a better understanding. That prayer was answered by way of Dawn's workshop.

The weekend was sunny and warm and the "Angel Workshop" was located at a nature center just outside the town of Slave Lake. I was extremely excited and very anxious as well; I felt like it was going to be life changing for me. I was not disappointed.

Dawn introduced us to specific angels and the hierarchy of them. I learned about energy and she demonstrated, once again, how she was able to connect. I was fascinated!

I recall sitting in this beautiful sanctuary, the final afternoon of the course, and suddenly feeling anxiety overwhelm me. Dawn was connecting to specific angels and she was giving messages to people. All of a sudden, she turned to me and said, "Archangel Michael told me to come to you." I instantly felt an overpowering surge of emotion and I burst into tears.

Dawn asked what I was feeling and why I was upset. I said, "I don't know". She went on to tell me that Archangel Michael was comforting me as I released some emotions that I had been holding onto for some time. All at once, I felt a calm come over me and my world was set right for the time being.

I attended the workshop with my friend Nancy and when the weekend was over we started our drive home. Along the way, we talked about what we had learned and then continued with the theme from the workshop of releasing emotions. We shared some of the things that had been bothering each of us.

While I drove, Nancy told me about a volunteer job she had just been forced to quit. The job was at this help center that was so important to her mother when she was alive, which made it all the more upsetting. I was supportive of her, agreeing with her analogy of the situation and the animosity she felt toward this one particular man who had forced her move on. Then, suddenly, my support impulsively changed. I began telling her in an almost lecturing tone that she had been unconsciously tied to this job because of her mother and *not* because it was meant for her to be doing. I explained to her that this man had been placed in her life to gently push her out the door for her own good. Nancy looked at me like I had lost my mind. It was then that I realized that right there, like a hologram floating above my steering wheel, stood her mother, with Archangel Michael standing behind her, just at her right shoulder.

I was still driving down the highway, fully aware and able to function. However, this apparition remained steady and clear in front of me. I told Nancy what I was seeing and she went dead silent. Honestly, I was in amazement and she was in shock.

I started to get really excited when I recognized what was going on and I saw Nancy's mom laughing at my enthusiasm. I spoke with this apparition for a few minutes more and then it was gone. Needless to say, the rest of the drive home went by very quickly and Nancy and I became connected like never before.

Nancy's mom came to me with messages again a week later, which I shared with her and then I seemed to be on a bit of automatic pilot for a few years, reading, learning and growing.

During the spring of 2013, I found out through being a member of John Edwards fan page that he would be in Edmonton, so I bought tickets and invited Nancy to attend the show with me. There were about 1000 people all rushing into the conference room at the Fantasyland Inn at the world famous West Edmonton Mall that September 11th.

We ended up sitting near the back of the room, but somehow I intuitively knew it was my turn for a reading. This time, I sat patiently and was very relaxed. After introducing himself and doing a little bit of an explanation about how he worked, he made a point of saying he was not the type of medium that ever talked about angels or butterflies.

John proceeded to do a reading for a family sitting in about the middle of the room. When he was done, he then moved to a couple at the far side, just across from us. He finished giving them their messages from their loved ones and then he came to our side of the room. He pointed to the back and said, "I have someone's son here". He went on to say the boy was about 6 years old and I stood up. I knew it was Travis.

Nancy had never been to see John Edwards before and she sat beside me very quietly. As his assistant handed the microphone to me, John gave me a couple of very validating messages and then went on to talk about an art studio. I told him that my family had just finished building me a cabin in our back yard to use as an art studio since I did paintings.

He went on to describe a painting I had done of stargazer lilies and said that Travis wanted him to talk about what was in the corner of the painting. I started to laugh when I told him that I had done the painting a few years ago, but it always seemed incomplete, but I had just recently painted a butterfly in the corner and now the painting is complete.

He looked a little stunned and maybe even a little perturbed at my boy when he realized that Travis had just made him talk about a butterfly, especially when the crowd started to laugh. I didn't have the heart to tell him that my signature in the bottom right corner was a blue Angel; it may have put him over the edge.

Literally only a few weeks later, I received a phone call that I had won a phone reading with John Edwards, again through the fan club. Talk about synchronicity and good luck! The day that we scheduled the reading was for February 20th, 2014 at 8 AM Alberta time. This was a perfect time since I had been following the Canadian Women's Olympic gold medal game and it was to start at 5:00 AM. I woke up excited for the game and after we won Canadian Gold, my phone rang to talk to John Edwards. Perfect!

This time, just like the last, Travis came through loud and clear. I think John may have been a little surprised that I wasn't more moved when he said he had connected to my son. Of course, he had no idea that he had already given me a reading just a few months earlier or that Dawn had connected with Travis years ago. I was essentially past the "shock and awe" of connecting with him and just wanted to get down to the message. It was a wonderful reading that lasted an hour and I feel so totally blessed to this day for my good fortune.

That same winter, I felt the need to attend some sort of conference or class or workshop about something, *anything* spiritual. So, I began to search the Internet and found an "I Can Do It" conference to attend in Vancouver. It sounded like the perfect weekend of listening to speakers such as Dr. Wayne Dyer, Sonia Choquette, Caroline Myss and Doreen Virtue.

I really wanted to go but not alone. I knew that Arlen probably wouldn't enjoy this kind of conference, so I asked him if he would mind me asking my beautiful friend Nancy to go with me. He thought that would be a great idea, although, his enthusiasm was probably relief that I didn't ask him to go with me. However, he did know that Nancy and I would enjoy it so much more.

She said she would love to go and it was awesome; two full days of enlightenment! I enjoyed the speakers immensely with my favorites being Bruce H. Lipton and Robert Holden.

During a break the first day, I was hanging out in the lobby taking in all of the excitement of the participants, watching people move about and purchase books and cards from the promotion tables. The energy was so uplifting and I could tell that life changing thoughts and moments were happening all around me. I saw a lady standing at a table who happened to catch my eye. She motioned me over and asked me if I was writing a book. This question startled me because I hadn't told anyone that I was in the process of doing just that. No one knew about this at that time, not even Nancy.

The lady told me that she works for a publishing company and also works with Hayhouse authors. We had a wonderful conversation, exchanged our contact numbers for the future and as I rejoined the others in the theater, I reflected on what had just happened. I decided I would take it as a sign to get at it; to finish my story, Trav's story, this story.

The rest of the weekend went wonderfully. We attended the conference during the day and then walked around downtown Vancouver, enjoying the shops and local eating establishments in the evening. We had wine and we talked about our days. It was perfect.

We returned home on the Monday after the conference and I was so inspired and walking in the clouds. I felt so uplifted, so light and positive. After a wonderful sleep in my own bed, I woke the next morning and was thinking "Okay, now what?" I knew I had to continue writing my book, but I also felt like I needed to continue on doing… what? Something else was pulling me, but I couldn't put my finger on it. For as long as I can remember, I would talk to God and my angels, but rarely would I take the time to listen for an answer. That particular day, an answer came in the form of a workshop.

As I was catching up on the wonderful world of Facebook, a friend of mine just happened to post about a workshop that was taking place in Grande Prairie a couple of weeks later. The facilitator was a lady I had never heard of, but I looked her up on her webpage and thought she sounded wonderful. I booked the class, told Arlen I was off again and went to my next adventure!

What an adventure it turned out to be. The class was a beginner mediumship class and I was very nervous, yet excited to be there. The Friday night started out with just a "meet-and-greet" introduction. I didn't know anyone in the class. There was one lady I recognized from High Prairie, however, we had never spoken before then.

The energy in the room was electric and the facilitator, Bonnie Wirth, was as wonderful in person as she appeared to be on her website. While I am rarely ever hot, the energy of the room had me almost sweating. Later that night, after the first session, a few of us met in the hotel lounge and traded stories and excitement. I met so many beautiful souls, so many enlightened people who were open to Spirit. After a couple of hours, I made my way to my room and tried to sleep. I was so excited for the next day that I had to do a meditation trick I had learned over the years to put myself to sleep.

The next morning and all through Saturday, I felt so much spiritually. It was like being at a Christmas Eve church service where everyone was happy and joyous and excited for the gifts they were going to receive. I was exhausted at the end of the first full day, so, after scrubbing and sanitizing (and scrubbing again) the hotel bathtub, I decided to have a salt bath.

I am *so* not a bath person, strictly showers for me, but I really felt like I needed to cleanse my body, spirit and somehow, my soul. I got the bath ready, put in some Lilac bath salts, added some more, since I had no clue how much to put in, then added a little more just because.

Over the past year or so, I had made a regular practice of asking Archangel Michael to cut any chords of spiritual attachment that I may be holding on to that are not serving my highest good. As I settled into the steaming hot tub, I decided to ask Michael to cut any chords of negativity I might be holding onto right then. I was sitting with my knees up and was bent at the waist, wrapping my arms around my legs. The steam surrounded my body and the lilac scent was strong. Something powerful suddenly came over me and I basically shouted in my mind for Michael to rip the chords of pain and negativity from my body.

I actually envisioned chords, thick and strong like vines of a tree, all being gathered into strong hands and literally being ripped from my body, from the center of my back. I felt it! I saw it! In my mind, I saw the space, the hole where the chords of negativity and the chords of pain were ripped away. It was amazing, it was exhilarating and it was exhausting! I spent no more than 5 minutes in that tub and my life was changed forever. I was so weak I could barely get myself out of the bath! I dragged myself to the bed and had the best sleep ever!

When I woke the next morning, I contemplated the events of the previous day and also considered what had happened to me during the bath that night. At breakfast, one of the ladies said that I looked different and I knew I did. I had released things that I never knew I had to release. It was awesome!

The Sunday class was powerful. As we moved through the day, we did an amazing meditation and had some fun doing "speed readings" as well as exercises. An epiphany happened for me that day; I realized, from listening to others speak about their mediumship abilities and readings, that I had been doing it for my whole life. Here I was, wishing, wanting, hoping to someday be able to connect with Source and I had been doing it all along! I just hadn't recognized it as such.

Actually, that is not completely true, I sometimes acknowledged some of my experiences as coming from Source, but I didn't really associate it with mediumship. So many times, something would happen and I would say after-the-fact, "I knew that was going to happen" or "I could have told you that". I didn't know *how* I knew, I just knew. I realize no that it was more than just intuition, which I often passed it off as that. Now, I know! I trust! I trust in my ability to connect with Source. I pay attention.

CHAPTER 10

Meeting My Team

I drove the two hours home after that class on cloud nine! I spent the late evening telling my husband all that had happened. As usual, he was so supportive and the next day, I dove in, head first. I knew I had to do it and I knew I was more than ready!

I posted this status update on Facebook:

> *"So I did something this weekend that rocked my world! I became a certified Medium! For all of you who would be willing to be practice clients for me, please message me. For all of you who are uncomfortable with what I do, please feel free to delete me from FB. I will honor my soul by following this path, and I honor you for following yours! P.S. Levi and Devon, I'm sorry, but you can't delete your weird mother, this is the New Normal! (You'll get used to it, I promise!)"*

I couldn't book appointments fast enough and WOW, did Spirit ever come through for me! It was remarkable! I did 4 readings the first 2 days!

I'm not sure when the realization struck but the thought kept popping into my head, that I had been somehow baptized that day in the tub. I had been cleansed and renewed. I had never lost God; he didn't need to be found, but that day... I Remembered. I remembered that God, Source is powerful and all loving! I remembered that I was worthy, that I was important, that I could trust and that I could create!

My first 2 readings were for good friends. I remember being nervous, but thinking, I've got this! It was amazing. I saw the family members of loved ones crossed and received a powerful message from one of my best friends' mom's. She actually lectured her daughter a little and I was concerned how her daughter would take it, but I gave it like I got it. Her daughter said that she needed to hear it that way.

I learned that day that I am not to judge what I am given, rather to just be the messenger. I had one job and that was to allow spirit to deliver through me, not to me. After learning this, it seemed so easy. I had people booking sessions faster than I could do them. It was wonderful and validating that I was on the right path.

There were so many moments for me where I was astonished along with my clients by what was given as messages. I could tell that my clients were more than pleased; some, most, were awe struck! I felt great and for the first time in my life, I felt like I knew what I needed to do, like I had found a calling of sorts.

One session I had really sticks with me as a reminder of how important it is to give the messages as I receive them and nothing more. A man and his wife, neither of whom I had met or even heard of, found out what I do through a mutual friend. They came to see me and I could tell instantly that the man was very anxious and that this reading was very important. I settled in and right away his brother came through.

The exact words I said were "your brother says there is a question regarding suicide", the look on the couples face let me know I had got something pretty important. The next thing I said was, "your brother wants me to tell you that it was an accident, that's all, an accident." I then went on to describe the accident in detail as I was given it as the man in front of me cried.

When I was done, the man told me how his brother had come to his house that morning after having an argument with his girlfriend. It was early and the man told his brother to come back later, the accident occurred shortly after.

The man then told me that he had waited 14 years to hear that! It gave him instant relief and peace. It was then that I really grasped the importance of telling it like it is, of giving the messages exactly as I receive them, without judgment or interpretation from myself. It is not up to me to say how the messages are to be given, that, I trust to spirit. If I had said, "your brother is here and I see a suicide" the message could have been taken totally out of context.

Another amazing reading I had included a Native Indian brave named Kiwan who came through to tell my friend, Michelle, that her horse, a horse that had been giving her a lot of attitude, was *his* horse. As he pounded his chest, he told me that it was his horse and that Michelle had not asked permission to handle him. Michelle said that the horse was often unruly and would just run wild in the pen, but other times would be calm and willing.

I told Michelle that when she returned home, she should ask Kiwan for permission to handle his horse and that he could even be called upon to help when the horse needed to be settled. First, she *smudged* the corral (burning sage) and then asked if the brave, Kiwan, was there; the horse nodded his head 3 times! Amazing! After doing this, she told me that the horse no longer has the same issues. She said she will even call on Kiwan to call her horse to her and the horse will come. Amazing!

I certainly don't have all the answers and I am learning every day. I sometimes get contradictions in my readings and it can be confusing. However, in the end, I just have to trust that what I am being given is what is meant to be given, what is meant to be heard by my client.

In the case of the horse and brave above, my mind is telling me that it is unlikely, even inconceivable to think that past lives could affect this life. I believe that we all exist at a certain frequency and that other lives exist in and around us that we are currently not tuned-in to. I should say, that we *chose* not to tune-in to, because all we have to do is focus on that frequency in order to tune-in to it.

I am still trying to wrap my head around the fact that we are not alone and that the whole space and time thing is irrelevant in the end, or that there is really no end. We continue from this life to the next, be it to another life on earth, a life on earth in a different time and space, a life in another dimension or forever with spirit. Our goal is to never stop. In fact, it is impossible to ever stop. We are constantly changing and moving and growing in energy. The laws of physics tell us that energy never dies; it just changes form.

The concept of moving from one time to another, be it to the past or from the future is staggering to me, but I believe we do. I believe that we not only have the ability to tune-in to past lives, but that we can tune-in to future lives as well.

You see, if space and time don't exist in the afterlife then, once we return to Spirit, moving backwards or forwards in time to interact in a new life experience is simply a matter of thought. It's like we can sit within the arms of Spirit, God, the Almighty Power, whatever you choose to call that Source and say, "I need to experience what it's like to live in a certain time and place" and then just *be* there. Of course, while we are in physical form here on this earth-plane of existence, most have no consciousness of the many other space/time realities that exist in the universe until they are revealed to us when we are in spirit form. I do believe some people are able to tap into certain times not of this plane. Our thoughts can easily take us there as well.

You see, I believe that there are different experiences going on all around us; like I mentioned before, it's just that we do not, or choose not to tune-in to that space/time frequency. This is why I have been able to connect to our loved ones who have passed. I found a way to "pay attention" and focus on a specific frequency that allows me to connect.

When people experience my interaction with spirit they are awestruck. They even praise me for it, however, I know that although I have found a way to pay attention to the frequency of what we call the afterlife, it is not *me* that is giving the messages. I am merely the conduit. I am not the one who decides or judges what to say. Not for one moment do I think I have that right.

About 3 or 4 sessions into my new adventure, I decided to sit down and write a contract with "my team". This contract is personal, but in essence, was a way for me to decide and put into writing some boundaries of where I would allow myself to feel comfortable with Spirit. I call my guides and the spirit that comes to give me messages, "my team". It has expanded to include 8 different and separate team members; however, I receive messages from the whole, from Source.

There may be others, I'm almost positive that there are, however, I trust that I am given individual personalities for certain team members for a purpose. Probably to satisfy my human need to connect to something with a name and personality.

I would like to share my first recollection of my first team member. I was meditating and all of a sudden I was walking along a path in the woods. It was beautiful, much like the trees I played in on my family farm as a young girl. As I walked along a path, I came to a bit of an opening where there were birds singing and a squirrel ran across the path in front of me towards a bench. Sitting on the bench was the most beautiful lady I have ever seen. I instinctively knew that she was an angel and I asked her name, she told me it was Ariel. She had very long, straight silver blonde hair and blue eyes. She was seated and I could see that her dress was a silvery blue.

The dress is so hard to describe just exactly as I saw it, because it was incredible and like nothing I had ever seen before. It seemed to be made of glass or light or soft, moveable silver. Both her hair and her gown sparkled like crystals. I walked towards her and said I was happy to meet her. She said she would be with me to help me. I don't really remember anything else except that I felt amazing; I felt so much love and comfort coming from her. It will forever be one of my favorite visits.

Ariel sits at my round table as part of my team. I introduce my team at the start of each session so that my clients know that it is not me alone who is working for them. It is also to give thanks to them for assisting me in connecting with the spirits of loved ones.

When I say round table that is exactly how I see them. I started out with just 2, then 3, then 5, then 6 for a long time and just recently, 2 more team members stepped forward. My table is not quite full; however, I believe that there are others around to assist in what I do.

One of my favorite introductions came from Archangel Raphael. The first time Archangel Raphael came through in a reading, one of the lights above me popped and went out. Now, I have two sets of track lighting in my studio; one set is over the area where I have my easel set up to paint and one directly above where I do my readings. Both sets of lights were put up the same day.

I didn't think anything about one of these going out, but then two days later, during another visit from Raphael and another pop; two lights down. The ceilings are quite high in the room, so I need a ladder to change the bulbs and didn't bother to change them right away. Then three weeks later, the very next time Archangel Raphael came through during a reading (you guessed it), another light blew.

By this time, I was thinking to myself, this is insane…a coincidence? I made a mental note of it, mentioned it to Arlen and when a week later and another visit from Raphael produced a fourth popped light; I knew it to be more than my imagination.

That evening, I sat and had a talk with Archangel Raphael and asked him from then on to please not blow out the light, to maybe just make it flicker. The fifth light in that track has not gone out to this day, almost a year later. I also have to tell you, the other track light at the other side of the room has not had to have a bulb replaced yet.

I've recently started working with children. I have parents who call me almost desperate for answers as to why their children are "seeing" things or feeling things around them. Often, I am told these kids wake up with incredible nightmares. Through my experiences, what I can tell you is that these kids are seeing and feeling the energy of spirit.

There are a growing number of children that are being born with an astounding sensitivity. One of the first things I do is to let the parents and their children know that they are in control; that they have control over what energies are around them. I tell them that they can ask the energy spirits to leave, plain and simple, "There's the door!" In almost all of the cases, the parents tell me their child no longer has trouble after that.

One other thing that I have observed is that there are so many children now who have electronics cluttering their rooms. Think about it, we are made of energy, and spirit is able to connect through our energy. In fact, as you sleep, as you rest, energy and universal knowledge are being "downloaded" to you. I also believe that uncomfortable dreams or nightmares are projections of things that we release and no longer serve us to hold onto.

Imagine all the interference there is if your child has a phone, a computer, electronic games, TV or even a clock radio in their bedroom. Do them a favor, remove the electronics or have a way to unplug them all when it is time to sleep. You would do well to look around your own bedroom as well; this doesn't only apply to children.

There are crystals, of course, that can also absorb the negative energies in a room and it is good to use them if you can't avoid having electronics nearby while you sleep. Black tourmaline works well for this but needs to be "cleared" frequently. Clearing is simply a matter of putting the crystal in dry sea salt for a day or so. The salt crystals draw out the energies that the tourmaline absorbed. Then throw the sea salt away (never reuse this no matter how tempting it may be).

Let's talk crystals. There are many amazing crystals and they have become very popular these days, even though they have been used for healing and ceremony in many cultures throughout time. They each hold a certain energy and vibration, even the rocks on a gravel road do as well.

If you are going to collect crystals or your children are collecting, it's always a good idea to know which ones vibrate at a really high frequency. It may not be a good idea to have a bunch of these sitting on your bedside table while you are trying to sleep. There are many, many resources available out there to let you know which crystals are good for what type of energy.

In all cases of energy, the most important thing to know is that you are ultimately in control of your environment. Always and in all ways!

I am still learning, I am still connecting with Source, with spirit during readings and I never tire of it. I ask questions and sometimes, if I am listening, I receive the answers. Most of the time, the answer is a variation of the same theme. The answer to almost any question is, "what you believe, truly believe, will be" This applies to everything, every-thing.

The most profound day of my life, the most life changing since the day of Travis' accident, came one day while I was doing a reading for a lady whom I did not know. I also did not know that she had lost a child. As I began my meditation to prepare for her reading that was to take place an hour later, I was granted another very special gift…

As I settled my mind and concentrated on my breathing, I began to call my team to the table. One by one, they gathered around and then as I looked across at Archangel Gabriel, he looked up with his striking green eyes and smiled at me. I smiled back and wondered why he looked like he had a great surprise or secret. I felt warmth spread over my right shoulder and as I tuned-in to focus on the energy, I found it to be extremely familiar! I was hoping and I had prayed and today, as my eyes filled with tears, my little man Travis stepped forward. He gave me the greatest hug and let me know that God had given him approval to act as one of my guides. "Hello mama," he said.

There he was, in all the love and light you could ever imagine. He was older now, not the little six-year-old boy with all the physical health issues he had while on earth. His body was all radiant light now. It was pure energy and yet I knew it was him, I knew his energy as if he was standing before me in flesh, blood and bone. I recognized his soul and that it had evolved. I felt and heard him communicate with me.

After my initial shock and awe, I immediately started to ask questions. "Are you Okay?" Of course, he was.

"Are you happy?" Absolutely. "Do you miss us?" No. "What?" He laughed and said he saw us every day, whenever he wanted.

Travis told me that he was so happy that I had let go of enough of my grief in order to communicate with him. I recognized the signs he had sent to me, trusted that they were from him, but this was different; this was a connection to his spirit-body, his soul.

I had done so much work over the last 16 years. It was 16 years of learning about who I was, what I believed and how to get to a place of contentment and then joy. I had studied and I had learned, but it was the *inside-my-soul* work that made the difference. It was the work I had done to let go of my old habits, of not feeling worthy, and it was the work of paying attention to what I *did* believe that made the difference.

I had found joy in a world that seemed unfair at times and I had moved through anger, forgiveness and unworthiness regarding myself. All of these things were so important to allow me to move forward on my path through life and my path to communicating with Travis.

I know I am not nearly done. I have so much more to learn, so much more to let go of and so much more to forgive. However, I also know that I am moving forward; I am vibrating higher on the path. And it is this progress that is leading me to find the joy in my life, which allows the shifts of energy that permit the communication with Travis. What a blessing!

It has been sixteen years since our son left this earth to return to heaven. It has been six hours since I last spoke to him! No, I'm not crazy; I talk to him every day. Whether it is just a whisper of "Hello", a long conversation, or sometimes he just crosses my mind; he's there, always.

Anyone who has lost a child knows what I am talking about. They never really leave you through the act of their physical bodies dying; our children stay with us in our hearts and in our minds, always. I am fortunate enough to have figured out how to be well and joyful enough in my life to allow my son to communicate with me. Let me explain…

I have found out, thank you God, that because we are all energy and we all vibrate at different frequencies, it is that frequency and the science behind it that allows us to be involved with, experience and communicate with our loved ones. Here's the trick, are you ready?

In order to communicate with your loved one, you have to meet them on the same frequency. It's as simple as that. Understanding that they are in a place where they are free from the emotions that hold us back, that we hold within ourselves as humans, means that they are most likely vibrating at a higher level than we are. So, in order to meet them in that great place, we have to raise our vibration. Sounds simple enough and really, it is. We have to live our lives in a place of joyfulness and happiness in order to rise to the frequency they maintain.

I have done multiple readings for people who are desperate to connect with their loved ones and they all have a similarity to them. Almost every one of these readings consist of people who are so tied up in their sorrow that they cannot see the signs their loved ones are sending to them constantly. They are trying too hard, they are wishing for too much and they are definitely holding themselves apart from the frequency they need to be at in order to see, hear and feel their loved ones.

I was there, I totally understand, especially in the first few weeks into your grief, where you can be so absorbed in your own sadness. The pain is so intense that it feels like it takes everything you've got to simply function; but you must. You must move into a place of feeling a little bit better each moment and eventually into a place of joy where communication can be realized.

CHAPTER 11

Let It Go!

S ue came to me only a few months after her husband died. She walked into my studio looking like she had literally been put through a wringer. She was dressed nicely and well groomed, but there was no light in her eyes, no color in her face and no shine to her hair; she was broken. Her heart was broken and her mind was thick with grief.

She took a seat on the couch and it seemed to swallow her as she sank back into the cushions. I felt her pain in my solar plexus. I felt her emptiness in my heart and I felt her desperation in my mind. I took a moment before starting the session to add an extra little prayer for *my team* to please help me bring some peace to this lady.

Before I finished talking to my guides, her husband stepped forward and told me he was there and he was well. He had a gentle smile on his face and so much love shining from his eyes; it almost made me cry. I was able to give some very specific examples to Sue about how her husband had been with her during these last few months.

I had never met Sue or her husband and asked her why he showed me 4 children walking with him? She said she had one miscarriage between her two children with her first husband and had 3 miscarriages with her second.

Her husband told me that there would be signs from them for her in the form of butterflies. She said she had noticed a lot of butterflies this year. I asked her if she saw a lot from the living room window and what was in front of the window, was there a chair? She said that yes, his big rocker recliner sits there.

Next, I asked her why her husband was showing me a piece of jewelry with a knot, like a rope tied in a knot. She told me that she had worn a necklace with a knot that he had given her; it was hid beneath her shirt and jacket. On her way to meet me, she had asked her husband to mention it if he was there. I was able to give her confirmation over and over again about specific things she had done the past few days and even what he thought about an issue a family member was having.

Sue sat, absorbing it all and I could see a little bit of the cloud lift with every detail I was able to give. It made my heart soar to witness the love between these two and as the reading neared the end, he spoke of a song he was sending her, actually, he was singing it to her.

She told me that she had no idea what song he was talking about, but that he had often sung to her; I told her that perhaps it would come to her later. I was given one more message for her. She was to "let it go". Her husband did not tell her to let *him* go, but he told her he wanted her to get up and let go of the anger and the debilitating fear that she was feeling with the loss of him. He told her that he wanted her to live her life to the fullest of her capacity with joy and love in honor of him, for herself. It was beautiful!

She seemed a little surprised by his message, as if she somehow expected him to be happy that she was still grieving and pining for a life they would no longer share together as a couple on earth. I ended the reading and as I walked her to her car, I told her about how the song "Let It Go" from the new Disney movie, "Frozen", had become an easy symbol for spirit to use with me letting me know when people were to "let go" of issues in their life. She said that she hadn't heard of the movie or the song I was referring too. She also said she rarely turned on the TV anymore and didn't really listen to the radio. It made me sad that she closed off her life this way and I wished her well, again, sending up a little prayer that she find peace in her heart.

A few days later, I received an email from Sue and it was amazing! She told me that as she drove into her yard and up towards the house after her reading, she was surprised to see 4 ornamental butterflies on the wall on the side of her home; she had forgotten they were there. She also told me that the next day, her niece had come for a visit and she had turned on the TV to see a children's choir singing "Let It Go!" Since then, it seemed like everywhere she turned, that song was playing. She also said that even though they had frost, she was still seeing an abundance of butterflies.

When Sue came to me for that reading, she was in such deep grief and despair that she could not witness for herself all the messages that her husband had been sending her. Her frequency was so low that he could not come down to her level, she needed to "let go" of the fear and frustration of being left behind so that she could return to a place of love and joy; he would be waiting for her there.

This is true in all things; we *choose* our vibration at every moment of every day. Therefore, we will only see those things that are at that same vibration; we will only hear what is at that frequency and we will only connect to those things at that same frequency.

Think of frequencies as being like horizontal lines and you are standing on the third line from the bottom. If you are focused only on what is in front of you, then that is all that you will see, ever. If you are standing on the third line and you are focusing your attention down toward the second line, you will eventually move down to that level; to that lower frequency. However, if you are always "looking up" from this position, you will eventually raise your vibration higher. It is law; it is the way of the Universe. Where you focus your attention is where you will end up. So, where are you focusing your attention?

My own life is wonderful now. I do personal readings several times a week. I do group readings periodically and I run a class for young adults called Spirit Kids.

I continue to attend Mediumship classes with like-minded souls and I am starting to facilitate my own adult classes. I love to teach and I love to learn. I am passionate about this world we live in and I am passionate to find out all I can about the sacred place we all came from and will all return to.

Spirit sends messengers to fill my days with awe and set me back on-track when I get lazy. As far as my soul, it is being rewarded daily with the energy work I do. A perfect example of this is a when a young lady contacted me via email to book a small family group reading. We set the date and all I had was her name, Rebecca. I didn't know her or any of her family that would be attending, or so I thought.

It was a Saturday in the spring and I was to meet my clients at my office at 3:00 PM. At 2:55 PM, four members of the family arrived, Rebecca, who booked the reading looked to be in her 20's. She introduced me to her sisters and her mother. I knew I had never met them before, but the mother looked very familiar to me. The next two people arrived and I had to take a moment to compose myself. As they walked through the door, I recognized one of the ladies. She was someone I had encountered throughout many years and one who I had gotten into an argument with a few years previous. We had a disagreement over how the disciplinary committee of our local hockey association handled a certain situation.

I quickly realized why I thought Rebecca's mother looked so familiar; she was a sister to the lady that stood before me now. I held my nerves at bay and ushered them upstairs to where I do my readings. As I took each step, I tried to calm myself as I asked God what he was doing, what I should do. I called on my team and asked that they give me the strength and grace to handle this situation. I was amazed that this lady had come.

At first, I was astonished that she even had the nerve to come into my place of business to meet with me like this, given our past, unfriendly communications; but just as quickly as the thought crossed my mind, my beautiful and loving team surrounded me with grace and love. My mind was cleared and I felt an immediate release of old, hurt wounds from my heart. I was able to give the reading with strength, grace and love, just as I had asked for. It happened that quickly.

When I returned home later that afternoon, my husband asked how my reading had gone. I told him about who had attended and he looked at me quizzically. He knew of my issues with the lady and wondered how I was able to handle it. I told him it went well and that I actually felt really good. He looked at me for a moment and then stepped forward to give me a huge hug. He made a comment about what a big deal it was, he knew full well without my having to explain, what this reading meant to me. We both understood that Spirit was giving me a gift that day while I gave the gift of a reading to my clients; Spirit gave me a gift of release and more forgiveness.

So, at the end of the day, while Spirit works with and through me to help connect people with their loved ones, Spirit works with and *within* me to guide me closer to my own forgiveness, understanding and light.

The year was 2014. It was a lovely day and the leaves were crisp beneath our feet as I led my clients on the path to the back of my property where my studio sat, nestled up against a backdrop of stunning fall colors.

A creek ran through the trees and you could hear the frogs croaking and splashing in the cool water. There were birds chirping out warnings as we neared, and a squirrel sat on a branch, watching us intently.

I had known my clients for many years and I was so happy that they trusted in my abilities enough to come to me for a reading. A few years previous, this lovely couple had lost two daughters at birth, their third and fifth pregnancies. It was heartbreaking for them and I felt their deep sorrow. I also felt a heightened sense of anxiety and anticipation.

We chatted about the weather as I opened the door to my little studio and walked in. Once inside, after looking at some of the artwork I had done the past few years, we settled into a small sitting area, which I had delighted in setting up.

All chatter stopped as I lit some candles and I could feel the air heat up. I knew that it was a big step for them to put this trust in me and I tried to keep my nerves at bay. I trusted spirit and I trusted "my team" to bring the messages through, but I was nervous about being able to keep my composure as I knew a little bit of their story. I desperately wanted to bring them some peace and I desperately wanted to help them heal even just a little.

I turned to them and started the reading. After going through my initial routine where I introduced them to my team of guides, I closed my eyes for a moment and took a deep breath. When I opened my eyes, I looked towards where they sat and told them "your beautiful little girls are here, in fact, they've been with me all morning."

I explained to them that early that morning, when I had stepped out of my shower, I saw little Hadley twirling around excitedly; her sister Ailsa, stood quietly behind her. I knew who they were immediately and, although they had passed at birth, they now stood before me at about the ages of 4 and 5. They told me that they were very happy that I was going to see their mommy and daddy that day.

After my initial shock at finding two little spirit girls standing in my bathroom, I noted what they wore and how they looked so that I could pass the information on to their parents.

While allowing Stan and Jodi a moment to collect themselves, I felt an immediate change in energy in the room and I went on to give messages about things that only this couple would know.

My very favorite part of the reading happened when little, dark haired Hadley with the green ribbon in her hair, sat on the couch beside her dad, looked up at him with the most beautiful smile and bright green eyes and said, "Ailsa and I really like the song you sing especially for us."

Jodi, the mom, looked over at her husband inquisitively. Stan sat there for a moment, looking straight ahead. I think he was trying to absorb what had just happened for a moment before he looked over at Jodi with tears in his eyes and told her about a song he had been singing to his daughters when he was alone, thinking of them. Jodi knew nothing about this and was as shocked as I was thrilled.

There are many people who ask me why they can't hear or feel their loved ones around them. I want you to know that unless you are feeling good and unless you are in a place of feeling good about that person, your grief, or your despair, or your anxiousness about it will always act as a block to them. Your loved one immediately moves to a higher frequency when they die, so in order to connect with them, you need to be meeting them "up there" energetically. Some people connect right away and feel their loved ones while they grieve and I believe that is because they are numb, so in actuality, the absence of feeling puts them in a quiet place where they can connect; much like meditation. They are not pulling their energy down at that point; they are just letting their energy flow with no resistance.

When I saw Travis' energy rise out of his physical body the day he moved from this world to the next, I immediately recognized what had happened. It was not because I expected it or because I was religious and it definitely was not because I was a better person than anyone else or favored by God in any way. It was simply that I held no resistance to the unknown; I feel no fear of death and I am confident that we will all join each other in a beautiful and loving place.

At the end of the day, as I lay my head on my big overstuffed pillow, I remind myself of all of the blessings in my life. I hope you to do the same. This life we are living is full of joy and love and we are so fortunate to be able to experience it. I am learning, every day, how to move forward with the intention of being present in my life, of receiving into my heart all of the gifts of my soul. What a celebration this life is!

EPILOGUE

Questions with Travis

"Good morning Travis. I would like to ask you some questions and am excited to hear your responses. Here we go, question number one, the day you died, when you left your physical body, where did you go? What did you see?"

"Good morning mama. I am so, so excited you are here, willing... spending time with me. I have to tell you, I am excited to know that you are willing to hear my story. I know you want to help others and I want to help others too.

"The day my soul lifted from my body, I saw a light. It was in the distance and it was faint, but at the same time, it seemed to glow with incredible energy. As I moved towards it, it seemed to get brighter."

"How did you move? Did you walk?"

"Not really, I kind of floated or shifted my energy and was just there. I thought about being closer and I was."

"Okay, when you got to the light, what happened then?"

"I remember looking back at you and dad. I remember that I smiled and gave you great love. I wasn't sad then. I know you were, but I wasn't sad. I knew we would always be together. After I faced the light, I kind of moved through a tunnel. It was bright, I knew it was bright, but I could look around; it didn't hurt my eyes.

"There was a man there; he said his name was Michael. He was really tall. I saw that he had wings, so then I knew he was an angel. He smiled at me and I felt really, really warm. Next, we went to this other place. It was like a hall. There were all kinds of people there. I saw a lot of kids. Some of them looked scared and I remember wondering why. I felt great! It was like going to school the first day and seeing all the new kids you were going to play with. There were adults there too. Even some of them looked scared. I don't think they knew where they were."

"From there, what happened next?"

"We stood in line for a bit, talking with other people and then a lady took my hand and we walked through these big doors. She said she knew me and that we would be friends. Do you know what mom? I could see without my glasses and the colors were so bright, so magnificent. I wanted to see everything. There was grass and trees and colors and colors and colors. As we walked I could feel the light under my feet. Oh yeah, I was barefoot and my feet didn't hurt anymore, they were perfect. I could see right through them, like I was invisible, only I could still see me. Weird huh? Now I know why."

"Why, baby?"

"Because where I am, you don't need to have feet; you don't need hands or a body. You can just be light. You can do everything or anything you want, but you're light."

"Okay, so back to the lady; do you know who she was?"

"No, she was just there to take me to him."

"To who?"

"Well, Him. There was this nice man that I got to talk to. He told me I was home now and that everything was going to be okay. He smiled and I believed Him. I wasn't scared at all. I bet all those other kids weren't scared after they met Him too."

"What happened to you next, bud?"

"I got to go to this place where they gave me a shower bath, but it was with light. It tickled me. When the shower was over, I was dressed in a gown. It was white and had long sleeves and went to the floor. It was real comfortable. Then I went to meet the other kids. There were lots of them. We get to play whatever we want and no one ever fights. If you want something, all you have to do is to think about it and you can have it. I'm never hungry here; I don't think there is food. I haven't seen any. We just rest and play and wait for more kids to come."

"That sounds like fun, but don't you ever see any adults?"

"Sure, they're all over. They read us stories and play with us. Sometimes, I get to meet the new kids who come here."

"Where is 'here'?"

"I don't know, it's just here; where I am."

"If I were to follow and learn the teachings of anyone here on earth, who should it be?"

"Truth, always follow your truth."

(At this point, I noticed a shift in Travis' energy; he seemed older and wiser as he continued with our conversation.)

"There is no greater discovery than what you create on your own. You know in your heart what truth, your truth is. You know in your heart, who you agree with and who you should listen too.

"It's fun to discuss things. It's fun to talk to other people about the things that interest you. It opens and expands your mind, your thoughts. You create in those thoughts. You think a thought and it becomes a thing that can create its own thought. Nothing stays still, everything moves. Nothing sits still, everything, everyone, every – thing moves. It's in the joy of moving that the creation can begin, that the expansion can move forward, that the snowball can increase in size and speed. Constant motion. Constant creation. It's fabulous! It's delicious!"

"What gives me the honor or the right to teach? Because it feels good and it feels right for me."

"That's it then, it is right because it feels good and it feels right to you. When it feels good, it is always right. You can teach because you have an opinion and your opinion may have value to another, in fact, it does have value to another, even if that other person disagrees with you. It's in the disagreement or the agreement that thought, thinking happens, ideas and ideals form and it is in those ideas that energy is created and it is in that energy that expansion continues. It's a process that never stops. It always continues. It will always continue, even beyond your reality, because it is all of source and source includes that which you know and that which you don't. It is everything."

"Okay, so what about mediumship? Why has it changed for me?"

"Because you have changed. You are connecting with Source. You are always connected with Source. There is no stopping it. It must continue. It must move forward, it must, it must, it must… it is law and there's nothing you can do to stop it. Nothing. It's why we are here; it's why you are here. To move, to expand, to engage and to observe and in the observation comes the experience of all."

"So, when I do my readings, how do I know I'm doing them right?"

"Do they feel right? Do you feel good doing it?"

(I nod "yes")

"Then where is the question coming from? You know you are doing good. You know when people feel joy when they have a session with you. You know when a session is complete, that they leave with relief and a better understanding of all that is. They open a door to more expansion; they release old ideas and become open to new ideas. That can never be wrong, that is expansion. A sense that there is something else we don't know about, something else to think about. To observe; to grow; to expand. You facilitate a time and place for them to allow a thought in that hasn't been thought before. It's fantastic!

"We love to watch them watch you when you are tuned into Spirit. We love to feel and see the wonder and the awe they feel as you tell them things you couldn't possibly know; except we can all know, every one of us can know. It's just a matter of tuning into the frequency of what you would like to know, what you would like to experience. It's that easy. Turn the dial.

"Wouldn't it be great if every person that came to see you knew how to do what you do?"

"Then I wouldn't have a job!" I laughed. "Yes you would. There are more people in this world that need or could use your wisdom to learn to tap into theirs. You could spend your whole life meeting new people and showing them how to do what you do."

"I want to do that!"

"Good for you. That's all fine and well, but I am here to tell you, you would get very bored doing the same thing your whole life. You are a creator, so doing the same thing, saying the same thing, day after day, year after year, would become very boring; very monotonous. You would lose interest. You would lose passion and interest very quickly."

"So what should I do?'

"Whatever you want, until you want to do something else. It's up to you. It's always been up to you. There has never been anything in your life that exists that isn't up to you. Do you get that? Do you truly get that? There is no other way; it is law. What you want, what you truly want, you will have. What you put your energy to, will come to you."

MAY 6, 2015

Today was so great. So much alignment; so many great conversations.

"Trav, are you there?"

'Yes, Mama."

"Is our book going to be successful?"

'Of course, because you believe in it, it has to be. This is your time; your time to move ahead, forward into the greatest things life has to offer. You are ready and dad is ready to experience all that is and so it will be.

"There is no greater gift than moving forward, no

greater love than what you are experiencing. There is nothing you can't do and nothing that can be done to you that you don't allow.

"I see great things for you because you expect great things. It works only that way; there is no other way. What you want, what you truly want will always be yours. There is so much wisdom at your disposal. All you have to do is to connect with source and all will be told, all will be given. It is law, it is abundant and it is yours.

"Today is the perfect day and tomorrow will be the perfect tomorrow... *is* the perfect tomorrow. There is no choice; each day is perfect in its creation. Each day is perfect in its love. God, Source, the Divine knows no other. It knows not how to be anything but divine.

"It is written that those who believe will forever be given eternal life and it is true, your life is eternal within the light of Source. There is no lack, only Divine abundance. It can be no other way; it is perfect.

"Your book is perfect in its entirety. It is so much more than you now realize. There is so much more to be done and it is done. You will find power and grace and love and light.

"Enlightenment and healing, love and grace for all who read your story, for it's in your story that their story can be told; that their story can be revisited and ultimately healed.

"This book is so much more than a story; it is hope and it is love; it is loss and it is found. There is light and dark… and there is light found within the dark. How glorious, how expansive, how believable! God is good and glory be to all who enter into His love, His light."

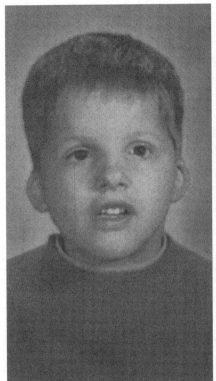

Made in the USA
Charleston, SC
01 September 2015